T0311571

Human Resources Management in China

CHANDOS
ASIAN STUDIES SERIES:
CONTEMPORARY ISSUES AND TRENDS

Series Editor: Professor Chris Rowley,
Centre for Research on Asian Management, Cass Business School,
City University, UK; HEAD Foundation, Singapore
(email: c.rowley@city.ac.uk)

Chandos Publishing is pleased to publish this major Series of books entitled *Asian Studies: Contemporary Issues and Trends*. The Series Editor is Professor Chris Rowley, Director, Centre for Research on Asian Management, City University, UK and Director, Research and Publications, HEAD Foundation, Singapore.

Asia has clearly undergone some major transformations in recent years and books in the Series examine this transformation from a number of perspectives: economic, management, social, political and cultural. We seek authors from a broad range of areas and disciplinary interests: covering, for example, business/management, political science, social science, history, sociology, gender studies, ethnography, economics and international relations, etc.

Importantly, the Series examines both current developments and possible future trends. The Series is aimed at an international market of academics and professionals working in the area. The books have been specially commissioned from leading authors. The objective is to provide the reader with an authoritative view of current thinking.

New authors: we would be delighted to hear from you if you have an idea for a book. We are interested in both shorter, practically orientated publications (45,000+ words) and longer, theoretical monographs (75,000–100,000 words). Our books can be single, joint or multi-author volumes. If you have an idea for a book, please contact the publishers or Professor Chris Rowley, the Series Editor.

Dr Glyn Jones
Chandos Publishing
Email: gjones@chandospublishing.com
www.chandospublishing.com

Professor Chris Rowley
Cass Business School, City University
Email: c.rowley@city.ac.uk
www.cass.city.ac.uk/faculty/c.rowley

Chandos Publishing: Chandos Publishing is an imprint of Woodhead Publishing Limited. The aim of Chandos Publishing is to publish books of the highest possible standard: books that are both intellectually stimulating and innovative.

We are delighted and proud to count our authors from such well known international organisations as the Asian Institute of Technology, Tsinghua University, Kookmin University, Kobe University, Kyoto Sangyo University, London School of Economics, University of Oxford, Michigan State University, Getty Research Library, University of Texas at Austin, University of South Australia, University of Newcastle, Australia, University of Melbourne, ILO, Max-Planck Institute, Duke University and the leading law firm Clifford Chance.

A key feature of Chandos Publishing's activities is the service it offers its authors and customers. Chandos Publishing recognises that its authors are at the core of its publishing ethos, and authors are treated in a friendly, efficient and timely manner. Chandos Publishing's books are marketed on an international basis, via its range of overseas agents and representatives.

Professor Chris Rowley: Dr Rowley, BA, MA (Warwick), DPhil (Nuffield College, Oxford) is Subject Group leader and the inaugural Professor of Human Resource Management at Cass Business School, City University, London, UK, and Director of Research and Publications for the HEAD Foundation, Singapore. He is the founding Director of the multi-disciplinary and internationally networked Centre for Research on Asian Management (http://www.cass.city.ac.uk/cram/index.html) and Editor of the leading journal *Asia Pacific Business Review* (www.tandf.co.uk/journals/titles/13602381.asp). He is well known and highly regarded in the area, with visiting appointments at leading Asian universities and top journal Editorial Boards in the UK, Asia and the US. He has given a range of talks and lectures to universities, companies and organisations internationally with research and consultancy experience with unions, business and government, and his previous employment includes varied work in both the public and private sectors. Professor Rowley researches in a range of areas, including international and comparative human resource management and Asia Pacific management and business. He has been awarded grants from the British Academy, an ESRC AIM International Study Fellowship and gained a 5-year RCUK Fellowship in Asian Business and Management. He acts as a reviewer for many funding bodies, as well as for numerous journals and publishers. Professor Rowley publishes extensively, including in leading US and UK journals, with over 370 articles, books, chapters and other contributions.

Bulk orders: some organizations buy a number of copies of our books. If you are interested in doing this, we would be pleased to discuss a discount. Please email info@chandospublishing.com or telephone +44 (0) 1223 891358.

Human Resources Management in China

Cases in HR practice

DOUG DAVIES AND LIANG WEI,
WITH CONTRIBUTIONS FROM XIE YUHUA
AND ZHANG XINYAN

CP

CHANDOS
PUBLISHING

Oxford Cambridge Philadelphia New Delhi

Chandos Publishing
TBAC Business Centre
Avenue 4
Station Lane
Witney
Oxford OX28 4BN
UK
Tel: +44 (0) 1993 848726
Email: info@chandospublishing.com
www.chandospublishing.com

Chandos Publishing is an imprint of Woodhead Publishing Limited

Woodhead Publishing Limited
80 High Street
Sawston
Cambridge CB22 3HJ
UK
Tel: +44 (0) 1223 499140
Fax: +44 (0) 1223 832819
www.woodheadpublishing.com

First published in 2011

ISBNs:
978-0-08-101714-2
(Chandos Publishing)

978 0 85709 1482
(Woodhead Publishing)

British Library Cataloguing-in-Publication Data.
A catalogue record for this book is available from the British Library.

Typeset by RefineCatch Limited, Bungay, Suffolk
Printed in the UK and USA.

Contents

About the authors

Doug Davies, PhD, is Associate Professor in Management and Head of the Management and Marketing School at the University of Canberra, Australia. His research interests are in Industrial Relations and HR Practices in China and Australia. He has taught in China, Singapore, Hong Kong and Malaysia. He has developed a number of professional relationships with universities in various parts of China, has published a number of papers, book chapters and articles on HR and IR, and is on the editorial panel of four journals.

Liang Wei is a Lecturer in the School of Business at the East China University of Science and Technology, Shanghai, China. She has lectured at MBA level for many years and has a strong interest in Chinese enterprise operations. Her wide contact with MBA students and her four years' experience in Chinese enterprises have given her deep understanding in Chinese businesses. She has translated several business books into Chinese and introduced them to China, and has published a number of papers.

Yuhua Xie, PhD, is Professor of Management and Director of the School of Business and Management, in the Faculty of Business and Management, at Hunan University, Changsha, China. Her research and teaching interests are in the areas of Industrial Relations, HRM, and Communication for Managers. She has published seven books and more than 60 papers.

Zhang Xinyan is a PhD candidate at the University of Canberra. She has published a number of papers in both Chinese and English journals and conference proceedings, as well as having had a book chapter published in 2009. Prior to coming to Australia she worked as a Human Resource Manager at Xinjiang Medical University. She was also successful in gaining a scholarship from the China Scholarship Council.

The authors may be contacted via the publishers.

Acknowledgements

We would like to thank the CEOs, owners, managers and employees of the various companies that gave so willingly of their time to be interviewed on their respective human resources practices, as well as answering any follow-up questions or clarifications we had about the cases that were researched. We would also like to thank our respective Universities (University of Canberra and East China University of Science and Technology) for giving us the time to do this research, and the publishers for picking up the various minor errors.

On a personal note, Doug Davies would like to dedicate this book to his wife, Christine, who endured my absences while researching in China, as well as to my children and grandchildren.

List of figures and tables

Figures

Tables

Introduction

The role of human resources in China has been developing over the last 30 years as China has moved from a command economy to a more open market environment. Although managers in many state-owned and private organisations managed their staff effectively, it was more at a functional and operational level than strategically. Loyalty between management and employees tended to be a stabilising factor in the working relationship.

With the opening of the economy to multinational organisations, the focus of the human resource discipline has been changing, with greater importance being placed on staff retention, motivation, performance and careers. As is demonstrated by the cases presented in this book, many employees are now more prepared to move to other organisations if better compensation, career paths, and training, among other job-related aspects, are provided. One of the major concerns of many companies now appears to be retaining staff with the appropriate and necessary skills.

Method used

This book is a collection of cases which demonstrate the changing nature, acceptance and growing importance of human resources in the newly developed and developing economy of China. This differentiation is made as it is considered that the eastern part of China is as well-developed as many Western countries, and the government is developing the inland areas of the country quite rapidly, through encouragement of investment and training of the population.

The cases in this book cover a range of human resource problems in private, state-owned and joint venture operations, with in many instances solutions which have been devised within the Chinese context or modified from other sources. All of the case studies in this book (with one exception) are based on original and empirical research, and were collected from a number of interviews held in various parts of China in 2008 and 2009.

The format of the interviews followed a semi-structured series of questions in which background information about the organisation was asked, followed by a specific problem or problems that had occurred relating to management or the human resources (HR) function. The solutions adopted by the company to the problems were then given and the results of these solutions, both positive and negative, were provided to the interviewers. The approach taken was to present a proactive stance on the part of the organisation to solving problems, to demonstrate how in many instances the HR practices are becoming very innovative and culturally specific. In a number of the cases, the policies may have been developed by the parent company in another country, but appropriately changed to suit local circumstances.

Despite the structured format of the questions, however, the respondents presented much material that potentially related to other questions. As mentioned below, this then required the editors to re-organise much of the material to ensure that it was presented in a logical sequence.

Cities visited over the course of the research included Shanghai, Beijing, Zhuhai, Xi'an, Changsha and Ningbo, and interviewees ranged from general managers to HR managers and other management or associated staff. Some of the interviews were in English, but many were in Chinese and needed to be translated. All the interviews were recorded and once translated, initially transcribed with the assistance of 'Dragon' software.

As much of the information collected was potentially confidential, the names of the organisations in all instances have been changed to ensure privacy and to protect the company (and the interviewee, if considered necessary). Also, the specific location of a number of the companies was altered, and a broad geographical location was given for these businesses.

The organisations consisted of a variety of solely Chinese enterprises, as well as co-owned and multinational organisations operating in China, demonstrating the more open market policy being advocated in the country. The cases are of varying length but do provide an overview of many of the problems that are occurring in the Chinese HR context, as well as giving a number of the innovative solutions that are being tried.

All of the case studies in this book were written equally by Doug Davies and Liang Wei, with the exception of Chapter 7, which was written by Professor Yuhua Xie of Hunan University, Changsha, and translated by

Liang Wei, and Chapter 15, which was written by Doug Davies, Liang Wei and Zhang Xinyan.

Literature review

Each of the cases has a brief introductory review of the literature, with the exception of Chapter 7. Chinese literature has been generally used in this book to provide some framework to the cases presented. This is not because of the shortage of literature in the west covering many of the cases discussed, but because of the limited exposure of Chinese research into HRM in many countries outside China. There was some discussion regarding this approach, but the authors thought it most appropriate to broaden the exposure of Chinese academics.

Issues discussed in the studies

There are 15 case studies of varying lengths included in this book, beginning with Chapter 2. Many HR issues are discussed, as well as some general management concerns to the companies, where raised by the interviewees.

Chapter 2 examines the need for a succession plan to be provided in an organisation, and gives the framework that was used to implement an effective and viable succession system due to the staff turnover occurring in the city of Shanghai. The issue of staff shortages is also raised.

Chapter 3 looks at the problems experienced by a furniture exporting company based in Ningbo, and the difficulties experienced by management in obtaining suitably qualified staff to work within the organisation. The issue of staff taking responsibility for their work, compensation and training issues are also mentioned.

Chapter 4 raises a number of HR issues occurring at a joint venture operation in central China. Problems discussed include staff development, cross-cultural problems, recruitment, remuneration and performance management, as well as industrial relations matters. Solutions that are being implemented are also discussed.

The airline industry is growing rapidly in China. Chapter 5 examines the relationships between the various stakeholders, and the difficulties in devising a suitable and viable airline and related organisational structure. Coupled with this is the difficulty in obtaining and retaining suitable staff, safety and occupational health matters, and employee loyalty.

Chapter 6 studies the HR impact of a merger and acquisition of two United States based companies with subsidiaries in China, and the effect on the culture of the acquired company. Training, staff reduction, recruitment, leadership, expatriate issues and industrial relations changes are raised.

Chapter 7 examines a number of performance and compensation initiatives that were introduced into a previously state-owned enterprise and the concurrent problems arising due to the acceptance of the change processes by staff. Performance-related pay is proposed, and the study provides more questions than answers on cultural change practices.

The balanced scorecard (BSC) has been used as a tool to more accurately assess performance within organisations. Chapter 8 examines the role of the BSC and how it reduced duplication of duties, thus improving efficiency, enhanced training, and focused on better staff alignment and improved communication and customer service.

Chapter 9 examines the problems of staff turnover following a change of management in a multinational company, with its headquarters located in Shanghai. Major recruitment was needed to ensure that the staff complement was maintained, with an emphasis placed on educating staff in the company's core values through more effective induction programs and cultural change initiatives.

The service industry in many countries experiences difficulties in retaining staff. The reasons include lack of job security, limited career paths, and perception of potential employees regarding the industry. Chapter 10 looks at a number of initiatives undertaken by a hotel in Zhuhai to ensure the motivation and retention of valued staff.

Chapter 11 examines the difficulties in attracting suitable staff to a business incubator in a small regional city in Guangdong Province. The initiatives used to attract suitable staff to the city and to provide training for existing residents, supported by the local government, thus raising the economic standing of the city are given.

Chapter 12 focuses on a Chinese-owned organisation which has had substantial success in retaining and motivating staff by adopting a caring approach to its employees and providing them with a safe and attractive working environment. Low turnover, high retention and high motivation have been the results coming from this approach.

With the increasing demand for staff with skills and qualifications in engineering and other technologies, many companies have difficulty in retaining staff due to the shortage of suitable employees. The company discussed in Chapter 13 is using remuneration as an incentive, with mixed success, through gain-sharing to attract and retain talented employees. Equity issues are an aspect that needs further consideration, however.

Chapter 14 examines the cultural problems that a foreign company experiences when it becomes involved with a Chinese organisation. The emphasis is on changing the culture, especially as it refers to safety and financial re-organisation. Resistance to the changes and solutions are given, which are adaptable to companies experiencing similar problems.

Compensation strategies are a popular tool in motivating and retaining staff within an organisation. Chapter 15 examines the changes in evaluating and remunerating staff in a manufacturing workshop located near Shanghai, and the different incentive systems used, and the problems that were encountered in the expansion of the business with it using stock options and gain-sharing plans.

Staff motivation and the relationship to performance and compensation are the core areas examined in Chapter 16, in which the organisation designs and implements a reward-based performance system. This system has the effect of improving staff behaviour, reducing customer complaints and generally improving the profitability through increased customer business.

The concluding chapter examines some of the trends occurring, and briefly examines a recurring issue, noted throughout the research and discussion with the interviewees, of skilled staff shortages in the most populous country in the world.

Succession planning in the Chinese subsidiary of a multinational enterprise

Introduction

Succession planning in an organisation results in a plan being devised to locate potential successors, review their readiness for the position and develop them for an appropriate role within the organisation (Evan et al., 2002). Unfortunately, despite it being an essential HR planning tool, succession planning tends to be only a second thought in many organisations, both small and large. Additionally, the academic literature and models on both succession planning and workforce planning (a close association) tend to be very scarce. In China, the literature focuses on Chief Executive Officer (CEO) succession, generally ignoring the other levels of management staff within the organisation.

This study is of a Chinese organisation that has realised the need for a succession plan to be brought in due to the increase in staff turnover in China as a result of the booming economy. The organisation is a Shanghai-based subsidiary of an automobile components manufacturer, which has its head office in the United States. The succession plan, though originally based on the US company's model, was modified to suit Chinese culture.

A modified framework, based on work done by Davies and Sofo (2006), has the potential to integrate a number of the key elements involved in the succession planning process. Many of these elements are becoming increasingly important due to the difficulty in obtaining suitable staff in a competitive environment (Turner, 2005). This chapter examines the differing aspects of a succession plan introduced to ensure stability into the management structure of the company and the problems that the plan could create.

Literature review

The concept of succession planning was developed in a time when people remained in the same job and developed a career path within one organisation. However, there is now the realisation that people will not only change their employers, but also possibly their careers a number of times in their working life (Leibman et al., 1996). An issue with this is that organisations may lose much of their aspiring talent and corporate memory.

Laff found that surprisingly few organisations had a formal knowledge transfer process in place, to ensure retention of corporate memory (Laff, 2008). This can have major implications for the company and could easily impact on customer loyalty and the financial health of the business. Research on succession planning and stockholder values has revealed that an effective succession plan is reflected in positive share market reactions when an internal employee, an 'heir apparent,' is appointed to a CEO position within a firm (Davidson et al., 2001; Naveen, 2006). This reflects on the positive financial impact of a succession plan.

As far as customers are concerned, when devising a succession plan, an organisation needs to decide who are the crucial people that would cause most disruption on their departure (Haserot, 2008). It is likely that a departing employee may take a solid customer base away from the firm or that patronage may decline due to new staff members not being sufficiently aware of the corporate culture in more senior roles.

It is imperative, therefore, that all organisations consider identifying potential senior managers; an effective succession plan is needed to develop this potential (Oddou and Mendenhall, 1991).

The problem, then, is how to identify potential management ability, as well as how to attract new staff into the organisation to develop further. Competency models appear to be an effective way of determining the potential success of candidates for a succession planning programme (Rothwell, 2002), and career development has been shown to be an appropriate mechanism for attracting employees into a company to develop into potential management and other senior roles (Younger et al., 2007). Depending on the state of the labour market, it may be difficult to maintain staffing levels unless some appropriate model is in place to assist in retention of staff. To develop a suitable model, appropriate leadership competencies need to be identified, and structures need to be in place to identify emerging leaders, not only in potential skills but in their loyalty to the organisation (Turner, 2005).

The staff retention issue is not only a Western phenomenon, although leaving an employer is becoming a more frequent occurrence (Kransdorff, 1996). This is becoming more commonplace globally as previously less-developed countries broaden their industrial base, with a comparable shortage of skills to fill the increased managerial and technical roles. It indicates that a good method of ensuring continuity in a company is to have an effective succession plan in place. This provides a pool of labour that has been trained to fill vacant positions as they occur. One area where this is becoming more prevalent is in China, especially with the entry of multinational companies and their capacity to provide additional benefits to their staff.

In China, much of the literature on succession plans is theoretical study. Zhang and Wei (2006) examined a number of articles related to succession plans in China and categorised these into three areas, namely pre-succession factors, succession process and outcomes after succession. They found that more than 80 per cent of the articles focused on theoretical research and frameworks, with research on actual practice and empirical studies being very scarce.

Due to the social system, there are a large number of state-owned enterprises (SOEs) in various industries in China, where the CEO succession practice is quite different from that in the Western world or in other types of companies. Dang Xiaolong and Zhang (2004) analysed the CEO succession in large SOEs in China from 2000 to 2002 and found that more than two-thirds of the successor candidates came from within the company, while outside successors mostly came from government assignments or senior management exchanges among large SOEs. As to the reasons for succession, Li Xinchun and Su Xiaohua (2001) found that the reasons why a CEO stepped down were mainly based on subjective criteria such as 'superiors or the public are not satisfied' instead of unsatisfactory company performance. This was interpreted by Li Xinchun as the characteristics of SOEs in a transitional economy, which still conveys a lot from a planned economy.

Besides SOEs, private companies account for an increasingly large part of the Chinese economy due to the changes brought to China in the 1980s. Succession issues have also become more and more important in a growing number of family-owned enterprises. Due to the influence of Confucianism, which holds family and blood relationship in high regard, a large percentage of family-owned businesses in China were taken over by family members. Zhu Suying (2006) conducted a survey among 128 family-owned businesses in Zhejiang Province, Southwest China (the most developed private economy area in China) on successor selection procedure and criteria, reasons for succession, successor origin, motivation of successor and time of succession in 2005 and found that the predecessor played a decisive role in selecting successors in 59.1 per cent of the companies. When selecting candidates, 48.7 per cent of the companies gave first priority to their family members. Consequently, 62.4 per cent of the successors came from within the family, while the remaining 37.6 per cent were promoted from within the company or were total outsiders. This was ascribed by Bao Fagen (2006) to greater importance being attached to commitment and loyalty, rather than to competence, by the family-owned businesses. Two other reasons for this are the relatively smaller size and less advanced technology of family-owned enterprises, and the increased familiarity of the founders' children with the company's culture, strategy and competitive advantages. However, Li Xinchun (2001) argued that it may not necessarily be harmful to business, due to those successors' better position to integrate their work experience, family cohesion and modern management approach.

Very limited studies were found about succession at middle management level. Zheng Aixiang (2007) suggested job rotation, job enlargement and acting as assistant to key positions as some practical ways of developing possible candidates. He also pointed out that companies needed to adapt their approaches when selecting candidates due to the nature of positions, and the personal qualities and needs of the candidates.

Ji Fuxing (2006) discussed four aspects of managing CEO succession: identifying the required value and competence structure of eligible candidates according to company's vision and strategy; conducting due diligence and comprehensive evaluation when searching for potential candidates; regular discussion and view-exchanges on the suitability of candidates within the board of directors; and a well-developed training and development scheme for the candidates. These four aspects could be applied to middle management succession as well. Similarly, Xiong and Wu (2006) discussed perspectives to assess successors' potential: identifing with the corporate culture and strategy; leadership qualities and strong motivation to achievement, interpersonal skills and conflict-solving abilities; knowledge about company's core competence and outstanding job performance; sustained self-development ability; strong loyalty and commitment towards the company.

The framework

A suitable framework based on a workforce planning model will integrate a number of key elements into succession planning. Training and assessment of performance, based on key competencies, such as leadership, dedication or loyalty, attitudes, teamwork, communication and innovation work, provide a suitable model for an organisation in planning for its leadership needs for the future. Other ancillary but important features noted from the literature are problem- and conflict-solving skills and the ability to continually develop. These provide the basis for a suitable succession plan for an organisation.

The organisation

OEO is a manufacturer of luxury products for automotive vehicles. It manufactures these products specifically for automobile interiors. Originally a company from the US, it was founded in the 1800s in Michigan as the Luxury Products Works. In the early part of the twentieth century it merged with the Subsidiary Components Company to become OEO. In the 1960s it became a subsidiary of TL Industries. Worldwide, it employs more than 4000 people and now has branches and/or manufacturing facilities in nine countries. Globally, OEO has 30 per cent of the world's share of luxury automotive products, and supplies its products to many leading automobile manufacturers. It opened its Shanghai branch in 2004 and now employs more than 800 staff, a mix of salaried, production and non-core employees.

The vision

The vision of the organisation is 'to be the most respected automotive interior solutions company in the world'. It is going a long way to achieving this vision due to its good management and pro-active HR strategies, resulting in the industry expanding its operations and gaining more customers.

The purpose of the organisation is to passionately pursue its customers' success through the creation of distinctive automotive interiors. The company is now the world's largest supplier of premium automotive products. Since their inception, they have consistently demonstrated a flair for the design of unique components – in skilled craftsmanship, unparalleled artistry and a focus on innovation. By striving to create the best, most luxurious product possible through applications support, research, and development, OEO has become the standard for excellence and refinement in the luxury automotive component field.

This is demonstrated in the adoption of their product by many leading car companies. This includes the components for car interiors, door panels, seating, and steering wheels for customers such as BMW, Nissan, Mazda and Cadillac. Their global market share is in excess of 30 per cent. Additionally, the commitment of their employees – to be the best in the world at what they do – has made OEO the most respected component manufacturer in the industry.

OEO in China

OEO commenced its Chinese operations in 2003. Due to its expansion, it opened a new building in 2005 and has continued to grow in operation since that time. It now has two plants in China, as well as offices in Guangzhou and Chongqing, and a subsidiary in Korea.

Each factory has a small HR support team. These teams provide HR and administrative support to the business manager in each area. This tends to be more project-based or focused on immediate employee relations matters. At the corporate level, the HR team is responsible for advising and providing the line management within the organisation with appropriate HR policies as well as consultation services. Assessments of management practices, strategies and solutions, are provided to the management.

Demographics

At the beginning of 2006, there were only 70 employees working in the organisation, but due to the success of the company, the numbers have grown rapidly to the current size of 800. Of these, salaried staff total 150, while 500 employees work directly in manufacturing and the rest are in the areas of maintenance, quality and procurement. Although there are two offices and a number of different workshops, there is only one supply chain line. All manufacturing is done in the Shanghai facility.

Succession planning

The company is considered to be very successful in its operation. Until 2005, there was no HR framework or policies. New policies and frameworks had to be devised to suit the expanding company. These included policies on recruitment, performance and training, as well as workforce planning.

The company realised that an important issue that needed to be addressed in relation to its staff planning was succession planning and the subsequent career development of staff. This view emerged from the realisation that staff were becoming increasingly mobile due to the economic changes occurring in China, especially in the large coastal cities. The decision was made that, because of this fast movement and potential turnover of qualified staff, especially at the management level, they would have difficulty in making the organisation run smoothly or systematically if there were no trained staff available to fill vacancies occurring as a result of resignation of key personnel, especially at the middle to senior management level.

The problem was deciding what training was needed and how suitable staff were to be selected for the training programme. Another issue was to determine how these staff were to be kept motivated and retained in the organisation if there were no immediate vacancies in which these trainees could use their skills.

Examining the succession plans from their head office in the USA, a framework of nine competencies was initially adopted, and a skills audit of potential staff was to be undertaken using these nine competencies. The initial audit of performance was limited to those managers at middle level and above suitable for possible senior management roles, and potential candidates were targeted. Each of the competencies had specific performance indicators that were used to assess each candidate.

The first step in the selection of suitable candidates had two predominant functions. These were to compare the candidates with the global behaviours indicator of the company, and to assess their leadership competency. These were measured on a scale of one to five. In the second step a panel meeting was held in which the HR manager, the operations manager and a line or panel manager discussed the candidates' strengths and weaknesses. Each candidate received a score and ranking. The third step determined the readiness of the candidates for the next position and the likelihood of retaining or losing them as employees. Due to the cost of the training programme, it was essential to determine the commitment of each targeted employee to the company.

A final review and discussion was then held to look at the overall organisation picture and decide on the suitability of the candidate to fit into particular positions within the company (organisational fit). This involved career planning for each individual who was selected to participate in the programme, and determination of the individual learning needs of each candidate.

Candidate selection

To choose potential candidates, two criteria were used. The first criterion was the candidate's current level in the organisation. To be chosen, the candidate normally had to be at middle management level. The second criterion was based on the potential candidate's performance appraisal review. If the candidate continually rated at outstanding, that person was likely to be chosen to participate in the programme. They were then further assessed in six additional competencies (see pages 18–20).

Learning needs

The HR department organised training and learning based on the individual strengths and weaknesses of the potential candidates. All of this training is focused on the individual learning needs of the trainee. These included:

- project assignments, in which the candidate was given a number of projects to complete;
- participation in a mentor programme – the candidate was assigned a mentor to provide them with guidance and advice as they progressed through the programme;
- various training programmes – the HR department designed a 'leadership passion facilitating programme' which was linked to the six competency framework. This programme consisted of a number of modules – passion for excellence, passion for people development, passion for stakeholders and passion for innovation and team-building; and
- job rotation, to provide the candidate with broad experience in other areas of the organisation.

The training format that was adopted is dependent on the learning needs of each candidate. A new temporary position was also created for each candidate to receive training and feedback from their immediate manager. In this instance, the supervisor was the mentor of the applicant. The functional skills were left to the line manager to identify, and appropriate training was given where necessary.

Job rotation was considered as an essential learning need to ensure employees were familiar with all aspects of the company. This allowed the employees to broaden their skills and knowledge of other operations, thus increasing their value to the organisation and further developing their appreciation of the practices and procedures used.

The programme itself was designed by HR, with support from the corporate department in its implementation. Fifteen competencies were adopted, nine focused on current performance, while the remainder focused on potential performance. To fit with Chinese culture, behaviour indicator definitions were created to suit the Chinese organisation.

Programme results

As a result of this succession planning policy, from 2008 the expatriate plant general managers were replaced by local managers graduating from this programme. This was a major cost saving to the company. Additionally, a job rotation system was introduced for production managers, so they could learn the different operations across the company. This has the advantage of the organisation being able to place a production manager into an emergency vacancy, such as when a manager resigns, retires or is sick for the long term.

The system has been modified and will continue to be modified to make it better. The organisation is planning to adopt a localisation strategy to train local managers to take over all operations. As business expands, this policy will be widened. For example a new plant planned for Thailand is to be under Chinese control initially. However, once staff are adequately trained in the process, localisation is to be implemented.

A further strategy is that the programme will cascade down to other levels within the organisation. Over time, candidates from lower levels of the company will be identified and allowed to participate in the scheme and develop their skills for future roles at the management and possibly technical levels.

There is always the fear that people who have been trained may leave if positions are not given to them promptly. The culture, however, is that if training is given to the employees, it will benefit the company and this will create more 'passion' in the employees towards the company. No contract is given as part of the training to ensure that people must stay.

There is also no commitment given to candidates that they will get a position. They are told to just enjoy the process and training given to them, and appreciate how it will benefit them and the company, as there are only limited vacancies that can be filled.

All potential candidates are advised that the training is part of their development within the organisation. This training, however, may lead to promotional prospects as the culture within the company is to promote internally, not get managers from outside. As the company grows, more positions will become available and the view is that they will have the qualified and trained staff to fill these positions. This is passed on to staff within the training programme to know that they may benefit from the increased growth of the market.

The competencies

Before 2003, there were only the nine competencies. The Chinese arm of the organisation maintained the nine competencies passed down from head office in the US, but developed six additional leadership competencies that were more related to the Chinese culture. The nine competencies retained within the framework are as follows:

Personal leadership – 'walks the talk'

This competency acknowledges the natural leadership abilities of the potential applicant. In this competency, managers look for an employee who automatically takes charge of a particular situation, and inspires associates and colleagues to follow their lead. This person may be obsessed with winning (which is a potentially negative aspect of the trait), but they also have a reputation and record of not giving in. This could be either a positive or negative trait for the company and the team; other aspects need to be brought in to temper the negative components.

A positive attitude – 'can-do'

A positive attitude has the benefit of being dynamic, infectious, and inspirational. In difficult times it can work to raise organisational morale. This attitude can demonstrate enthusiasm in the job and provides a high level and appropriate tone of service with internal/external customers, colleagues, and co-workers.

People development – 'teaches, develops and motivates'

People development skills demonstrate aggressive personal growth and can set challenging performance standards while respecting the dignity and uniqueness of each individual. This trait also proves an ability to share knowledge and experience with other staff, a valuable trait in a manager, especially when new staff enter the company.

Communication – 'shares ideas, listens and communicates'

Managers look for an employee who shares ideas and information with colleagues, listens and communicates with customers to gain a first-hand feel for the business. This is considered to be one of the most valuable skills that a manager of people needs to have.

Integrity – 'does the right thing – "ironclad"'

A manager should have the highest personal standards of ethics and integrity. They must also earn the trust of co-workers, and work to maintain the confidence of their team.

Diversity and teamwork – 'works collaboratively and values teamwork'

This trait enables the manager, by embracing and leveraging the diversity of his/her staff, to get the optimum performance level from them. This trait works towards attracting and developing the diverse talent that exists within any team. Additionally, it helps commit staff towards team-oriented behaviour.

Speed and innovation – 'works quickly and tries new ways'

This trait determines those employees who are energetic and who have a clear sense of urgency and direction. It also picks those employees who have a willingness to change in a positive direction for the company, those who are skilled at interacting and desiring change. In this trait, the focus is on doing everything simpler, faster and better for competitive advantage. This person establishes and relentlessly pursues positive goals to drive innovation and growth.

Passion for our business – 'lives OEO values'

Potential managers within the organisation must have a passion for the work that the company does. This passion demonstrates a pride in the employees, the processes, the product and the heritage. These people promote the company by their actions and positive approach, and they accept responsibility for ensuring that the company's good reputation is maintained.

Unsurpassed customer service – 'drives to be the best'

The extent to which an employee strives towards a goal and is successful in *knowing and building* relationships, and *connecting* with both their external or internal customers more than anyone else, demonstrates their commitment to always achieve the best.

Six additional leadership competencies were developed to suit the local conditions.

Achieve business excellence

In this competency, the employees demonstrate that they have proactively sought information on trends and issues, and that they understand the implications for their own area of responsibility. They need to demonstrate a knowledge of relevant issues – customers, markets, products/services, suppliers, competition, technology trends, economic drivers and financial indicators. They should also stay abreast of current advancements and changes by participating in various learning opportunities.

To further their entry into the programme they need to demonstrate unsurpassed customer service in their daily work environment. This requires them to continually raise performance standards and strive for superior performance in a fast-paced environment. Demanding goals need to be set with measurable performance standards and a continuous improvement focus. They need to strive to be the best by going beyond what is expected. Finally, they need to find ways to add personal value.

Creativity/innovation

The employees chosen for the programme must have mental flexibility: the ability to grasp new or unfamiliar concepts quickly, be curious and have an open-minded approach to problems. In their daily work they need to generate innovative ideas and solutions, identify critical high pay-off strategies, challenge the 'way it has always been done' and desire to continuously learn and develop both themselves and the organisation.

They must also have the ability to deal with abstract concepts and complexity effectively, breaking down a situation or problem into meaningful components. This allows them to tackle large projects in a systematic way. They must also learn from past experiences and apply this knowledge to current situations. When solving problems, they must evaluate alternatives, calculate risks and make well-informed and timely decisions.

Leadership skills

Leadership skills require effective communication as one of the key attributes of a manager. Employees entering this scheme need to communicate with impact. They must hold themselves accountable for the things they do, provide appropriate direction to staff under their control, lead courageously and command respect within the organisation. To do this they need to have excellent interpersonal skills, the ability to influence and inspire others, foster teamwork, motivate and empower others, coach and develop others, champion change, and attract and develop outstanding people from diverse backgrounds.

To do these tasks effectively, they must draw on the expertise of people within and external to the organisation and encourage people's abilities to achieve goals and strategies. To do this, it is necessary to establish an environment of mutual respect and trust, and create an organisation that values development. They need to surround themselves with talented individuals and use appropriate processes to reward and recognise achievement. To do this effectively, they need to be amenable to diverse views and value this difference of opinion prior to making a decision. Finally they need to behave both ethically and professionally, to protect the organisation's reputation and best interests.

Business knowledge

To be eligible to join the programme, the employee must understand the organisation, the industry and its competition, and analyse the impact on the business of the competition. To do this the employee must know the customers and the customers' needs and requirements. They must also have an in-depth knowledge of how the company works and appreciate the culture and history of the business and its value to the customer.

Within the knowledge of the business they need to have an understanding of corporate finances. They need to understand the financial impact of their decisions and use quantitative information to assist them in managing and making decisions.

Vision and purpose

They need to have the ability to impart the company vision into understandable terms for others within the organisation. Strategies then need to be created that are linked to the vision. These strategies then need to be translated into clear objectives and tactics that will result in organisational improvement.

To do this effectively, the manager must be able to align people, processes and organisational structures with the strategic direction, which will lead to the accomplishment of the vision. This would lead to inspiring buy-in and commitment to a shared vision and purpose of all employees.

Functional competency

The employee's functional competencies need to be evaluated to ensure that they are applicable as they relate to the incumbent's scope of job responsibilities in their current position. These competencies can be in a number of areas (finance/legal, operations, sales and marketing, engineering, human resources/administration, procurement/planning and information systems).

Measurement of the competencies

To ensure that the competencies were adequately assessed, performance indicators were applied to each of the 15 leadership attributes. They were measured under five standards. These standards are:

1. *Exceptional* – consistently exceeds job requirements and expectations.
2. *Outstanding* – consistently meets and often exceeds job requirements and expectations.
3. *Good* – consistently meets job requirements and expectations.
4. *Provisional* – does not always meet job requirements and expectations.
5. *Unsatisfactory* – demands immediate improvement.

These standards were then weighted under the achievement of set objectives. Candidates were ranked from exceptional, if they completed 150 per cent or more of their objectives, down to unsatisfactory, if they completed less than 60 per cent of their objectives.

Although the standards are quite stringent, as a succession plan requires substantial investment on the part of the company, it was considered that the cost was beneficial to the organisation if suitable potential and future managers were located.

What was learnt?

Sometimes there was some conflict with the competencies within the Shanghai facility. Some confusion resulted from their meaning and the grading system that was incorporated to evaluate potential managers. A review of the wording was examined to clarify this communication issue.

Another aspect of the programme is that it fails to adequately address the problem of staff being trained to a certain skill level but not being able to utilise these skills. This may lead to these trained staff becoming a valuable asset to an outside company. The temptation to leave and work for an organisation in which their skills may be better valued and used is of potential concern. This is especially so in the dynamic Chinese market, and is an issue that needs to be addressed.

Conclusion

This study has examined the increasingly important role that succession planning is playing in Chinese organisations, especially multinational enterprises. Although not a perfect plan, the management of the organisation realise that they need to have in place a contingency model to ensure that productivity of the company will not be compromised in instances of staff departure, especially at the senior management level.

Additionally, realising the escalating cost of expatriate management, they have put in place a localisation strategy to ensure that local staff gradually are trained to fill the senior roles. To ensure that the system is congruent with the Chinese culture, some essential modification has taken place to address the different expectations of management in China.

Finally, as a component of workforce planning, the approach should work towards maintaining profitability and productivity for the company. In the competitive market economy, this is deemed to be essential.

References

Bao Fagen (2006) 'Succession management and innovation: foundation of long-term development of family-owned businesses', *Rural Economy*, 4: 31–5.

Dang Xiaolong and Zhang De (2004) 'A study on CEO succession in Chinese large state-owned companies', *Journal of Tsinghua University (Philosophy and Social Sciences)*, 19(1): 59–64.

Davidson, W.N., Nemec C. and Worrell D. (2001) 'Succession planning vs. agency theory: a test of Harris and Helfat's interpretation of plurality announcement market returns', *Strategic Management Journal*, 22(2): 179–84.

Davies, D. and Sofo, F. (2006) 'Work-life balance: a critical outcome of strategic workforce planning', *International Employment Relations Review*, 12(2): 1–8.

Evan, P., Pucik, V. and Barsoux, J. (2002) *The Global Challenge: Frameworks for International Human Resource Management*. New York: McGraw-Hill Irwin.

Haserot, P. W. (2008) 'Breaking down silos, ending resistance, avoiding disruption', www.pdcounsel.com/Solution-multi-generational-challenges-succession-planning.

Ji Fuxing (2006) 'A study on CEO succession', *Journal of Scientific Decision-making*, 1: 53–5.

Kransdorff, A. (1996) 'Succession planning in a fast-changing world', *Management Decision*, 34(2): 30.

Laff, M. (2008) 'Knowledge walks out the door', *T+D*, 62(1): 20.

Leibman, M., Bruer, R. A. and Maki, B. (1996) 'Succession management: the next generation of succession planning', *Human Resource Planning*, 19(3): 16.

Li Xinchun and Su Xiaohua (2001) 'CEO succession: Western theories and Chinese practice', *Management World*, 4: 145–52.

Naveen, L. (2006) 'Organisational complexity and succession planning', *Journal of Financial and Quantitative Analysis*, 41(3): 661.

Oddou, G.R. and Mendenhall, M.E. (1991) 'Succession planning for the 21st century: how well are we', *Business Horizons*, 34(1): 26.

Rothwell, W. J. (2002) 'Putting success into your succession planning', *Journal of Business Strategy*, 23(3): 32.

Turner, P. (2005) *HR Forecasting and Planning*, CIPD, London.

Xiong Lian and Wu Shaoqi (2006) 'Evaluation of the potential of company successors', *Small and Medium-sized Enterprises*, 4: 28–9.

Younger, J., Smallwood, N. and Ulrich, D. (2007) 'Developing your organisation's brand as a talent developer', *Human Resource Planning*, 30(2): 21.

Zhang Wenxian and Wei Haiyan (2006) 'A study on researches of succession issues in family-owned enterprises in China', *Management Review*, 18(2): 31–5.

Zheng Aixiang (2007) 'Succession planning management', *Enterprise Management*, 4: 84–5.

Zhu Suying (2006) 'Zhejiang family business succession diagnosis', *Collected Essays on Finance and Economics*, 7(4): 96–100.

Staffing issues in a furniture exporting organisation in Ningbo

Introduction

This chapter examines the problems of a furniture exporting company located in Ningbo, a major shipping port near Shanghai. Along with many other companies in the eastern part of China, there are problems in finding suitably qualified staff to work in the organisation. Staff, when hired, can be difficult to train, or they do not wish to take responsibility for their work. They may state that the workload is more difficult than anticipated and then try to obtain a salary increase to compensate, even though they had been made aware of the job requirements prior to commencing. This action on the part of the employees is done in the knowledge that there is a skills shortage in the area, which places them in a good bargaining position.

Although the manager stated that this type of behaviour is not uncommon in this privately-run organisation, individual examples are given of some instances where this has occurred. Despite negotiations with staff to provide adequate training and compensation, in this company they have still tended to have problems over a range of human resource-related areas, from recruiting to motivation and getting staff to take ownership and responsibility for their work.

Literature review

Recruiting strategies vary between different corporations and for the level of the position that needs to be filled. Corporate culture, business strategy, the developmental stage of the company, and recruiting costs are all factors that need to be considered at the corporate level when recruiting staff (Sun, 2009).

An analysis of the Fortune 500 enterprises reveals that these companies have something in common in their recruiting philosophy, strategy, and criteria. They all attach great value to the corporate vision and strategy, with an emphasis on linking organisational growth with personal development. They tend to prefer internal promotion to external recruitment, while at the same time adopting multiple recruiting channels and techniques. Meanwhile, they all value person–culture fit in recruiting and put more weight on personal competence and qualities instead of educational background or experience (Li and Wang, 2006).

Huang (2006) proposed three perspectives to evaluate person–culture fit in recruitment, namely, honesty to the organisation, commitment to the position, and compatibility with colleagues. These qualities can be assessed through asking a number of casual questions in the interview about the candidate's life and job, through well-designed and validated multiple choice questions relevant to the three perspectives, and through written responses to open questions.

Apart from person–culture fit, Fan (2007) suggested that organisations consider appropriate person–job fit, person–team fit and person–organisation fit in recruiting. To achieve this, appropriate indicators and assessing techniques must be adopted to determine how a candidate's professional knowledge, experience, skills and achievements match the position and to what extent their qualities are compatible with or complementary to the existing members. Luo et al. (2009) raised similar views of position–demand fit, position–competence fit, culture–person fit and organisation–person psychology fit. Deng (2006) proposed the 3Q model in recruitment, namely, IQ, EQ and TQ (team quotient).

To achieve a good person–organisation fit, recruiters must ensure that a candidate's knowledge, skills and abilities match the job requirements, and the candidate's personality, needs and values fit into the company's culture. To do that, providing realistic organisational previews to candidates and necessary training to interviewers are both crucial. The appropriate matching level is contingent on positions, the developmental stage of the company, and its external environment. For instance, when an organisation is at start-up stage or in a stable environment, a high matching level is required, but if the organisation is mature or in a volatile environment, low matching may be necessary to encourage innovation (Fan and Dai, 2004).

Successful recruitment contributes a lot to Toyota's implementation of its strategy. Toyota closely links recruiting to its strategy of lean production, and extends its requirements from job description to enhancements of the core competence of the company, such as adaptation, flexibility and willingness to learn continuously. Besides this, Toyota try to ensure the involvement of job candidates through realistic job previews, and factory visiting by potential interns, which allows the candidate enough time to decide whether Toyota is their final choice of employer (Wang, 2009).

Corporate reasons may exist for the failure of a new recruit. For example, time pressure on HR to fill a position, and lack of orientation and training to help the new recruit to blend into the organisation smoothly (Wang and Wang, 2006). In addition, reference checks, role-playing in a pre-setting situation and psychological tests are potentially effective ways to ensure a candidate's personal integrity in the recruiting process (Peng and Huangpu, 2007).

The organisation

The organisation is a furniture exporting company that contracts orders to a number of manufacturers, checks the quality of the finished product, and then arranges for that product to be delivered to the customer, normally an overseas buyer. It has a number of other functions in addition to these basic roles, as do many other exporting companies. Broadly speaking, however, the organisation has two areas of responsibility.

The first is office organisation, the second is business organisation. Much of the work done is routine in which staff are required to perform certain tasks involved with the administration and the reorganisation of the office environment, as well as filling orders when required. The main duties of the office are looking at incoming and outgoing orders and requests, looking after the office cleaning requirements, and ensuring that banking and finance activities are undertaken on a regular basis. The responsibility for these tasks normally falls on one or two people in the office environment.

The core business of the organisation, however, is to contract with factories to manufacture outdoor furniture based on customer demands. There are 200 to 300 different types of furniture provided by the organisation, to suit different seasons and countries. This furniture is normally made in a batch from December to June. Other items manufactured by the company's contractors include paper items such as paper bags, gift bags, home decorations, and the third aspect of the organisation supplies sundry items such as kitchen furniture, kitchen implements and other associated items. These might include small household gifts or other small items that may be of use around the home. These are the three major areas that the organisation is involved in.

An additional responsibility that is undertaken by the company is to do research to determine current and future customer needs. It does this by maintaining constant contact with customers to determine if goods were suited to their needs, and what may be their future demand requirements. Within the company there are three merchandisers, who do this customer research work themselves.

The organisation also has a customer service division, which has the duty, among others, to handle customer complaints. Any problems that may arise are taken care of by the customer service division of the organisation, to reduce customer complaints and to foster the image of a reliable supplier. This division of the company also provides advice to the customers on ways to improve their home and living areas. This is part of the continuous service and customer improvement philosophy of the company.

The problems

A number of problems exist in the company, many of them being recurring matters. Every month, a meeting is held to discuss the problems or issues that may have arisen within the organisation, or any problems that may have occurred during the past months that may still need attention. Additionally, problems that may have been resolved will be discussed to ensure that they do not recur in the future, through examining what was done for the resolution.

However, with the growing number and variety of people working for the organisation as a result of its expansion, staffing problems are increasing. It has become more and more difficult to recruit suitably qualified staff and to control these people working in the company. There are a number of things in the work environment that have been causing dissatisfaction to some members of staff. These include aspects of salary and whether or not the organisation is paying a fair salary for the work that is done by the staff, and whether or not the employees are truly satisfied in the work environment.

Staff satisfaction

The matter of staff satisfaction in the organisation falls on the supervisor of the staff to ensure that the employees are productive and content in the day to day duties that they are undertaking. Unless staff are both productive and content, the organisation has both financial and morale problems to resolve. Some of the main issues facing the company in this respect are motivation and responsibility.

Management are continually researching to determine a better way to motivate staff and to get them to take responsibility for their day to day work. Many of the staff members feel that they are not paid sufficiently for the work that they are required to undertake. This brings in the money motivation factor and whether the company needs to review the wage structures in the organisation. This wage issue may also point to a problem in staff recruitment, mentioned later in this chapter. A related aspect is the area of responsibility, with staff not prepared to take responsibility for what they are doing. This, therefore, can become an ongoing problem for managers within the organisation, especially for those supervisors whose role is to motivate and trust staff.

The organisation does have problems in hiring new staff to work for them. Although it is easy to find and hire new unskilled staff, it is very difficult to hire adequately trained staff to work within the company. The company is very flexible in its approach to hiring staff, and will provide training if these recruits show potential, but the difficulty is finding staff that are prepared to take responsibility for the work they do. For example, recently a staff member resigned and the company was looking for a replacement. A number of customer complaints were filtered down to the manager, based on this employee's general attitude to customer service. She had also been causing a number of other customer-related problems and was continually making mistakes in her day to day work. The company was fortunate enough that the employee left without too much pressure being brought on them to dismiss her, with all the problems that might have been caused by this forced termination.

The replacement staff member had approximately six years of experience working in the outdoor furniture industry. One of the first duties of the new employee was to finalise many of the orders that the previous employee had allowed to lag. These late orders had caused a number of customer complaints to build up over a period of time. A number of problems arose, however, in that several of the current staff still had to be kept within the organisation for continuity. It was not an option to dismiss other staff as well due to the difficulty in finding suitable replacements. Coupled with this, a new factory was taking over the manufacture of the furniture and it was required as a back-up to the old factory, to ensure that sufficient furniture was being manufactured to cope with the increased demand from the organisation's customers. To ensure that the new staff member did not inherit too many of the problems that were handed down within the organisation, the supervisor offered to take over many of the old order problems herself and to resolve them so that the new employee was effectively given a clean slate to work with.

A brief induction, including some basic training, was given to the new employee, which took the form of allowing her to follow the supervisor in order to understand what duties were required within the organisation. The new employee was then given the task of managing the new indoor furniture division of the company, whereas the previous employee had managed the outdoor furniture division. It therefore took the new employee a reasonable amount of time to learn and to undertake the new tasks required of her, dealing with indoor furniture as opposed to outdoor furniture.

However, one day the new employee came to talk to the supervisor about an issue that was occurring. She had only been working for the organisation for 10 days. This employee considered that, in the short period of time that she had been working there, the work was substantially more than she had originally imagined it to be. She considered that the workload was excessive as compared to her previous employment, even though she was being paid a higher salary compared to her previous position.

This new employee was considering whether it was worthwhile remaining with the company due to this higher workload and responsibility. The employee therefore stated that, due to the work she was expected to do, she wanted a salary increase to be given to her of up to 3,000 RMB a month.

The supervisor initially thought about it and analysed the implications of this request for an increase in salary. These included the possible follow-on effect to other staff members. The matter was then discussed with her senior manager. Due to a shortfall in operating surplus at that time, a counter-offer was made. This was for the new employee to work for two months at only 2000 RMB a month increase in salary, and after those two months, once cash flow improved, they would consider giving the employee the 3000 RMB a month salary increase.

The employee was reluctant to accept the reason given to her so the supervisor explained a number of the problems that were occurring within the industry. The employee was told that if her work level was satisfactory over a 12-month period, the company would strongly consider giving her a pay rise because of the value the company placed on its employees.

She was advised that if she could do a good job and there were no complaints within a certain time frame, the issues she raised would be discussed at a later date. The employee, however, was still reluctant to agree to the terms given. She was threatening to resign if her demands were not met by the company. In addition to potential future salary increases, then, the possibility of a bonus was mentioned to the employee as another counter-offer.

The company stated that they did not want to lose those employees who were effective and good workers. As a result of this, her performance would be reviewed and an adequate reward would be given. If the employee could prove that she could do the job with no major complaints and no problems occurring similar to those caused by her predecessor, further discussion would be undertaken in the near future. Unfortunately the employee demanded the money first, refusing to accept the arrangement discussed.

The manager of the organisation then entered the discussions. Many of the employees considered speaking with a 'boss' to be a privilege and an honour. This was because the manager was a foreigner in China, and substantial respect was given as a result of this status. They were more prepared to accept the word of the manager than that of the immediate supervisor.

Although the manager, an expatriate from Germany, gave a substantial amount of autonomy to his supervisors, it was still necessary for him to intervene in certain circumstances. This was one of those instances. Although he took overall responsibility in the company, he did not stipulate what should be done, or what was the right or best decision. He was very much in favour of self-improvement and supported the decisions of his staff.

The end result of the issue was that the employee did decide to leave. She had worked in a factory before, but not in a wholesale or supply outlet. Her skills, therefore, were not up to the new tasks required of her and she was not prepared to learn and take responsibility for these new tasks. She was not capable of doing the additional tasks required of her. She was also not prepared to learn the additional skills, only being prepared to do tasks similar to what she had done before. The job, therefore, was above her current level of competence. She did not know what was urgent, and did not know how to prioritise her work and the orders. It was obvious that a wrong recruitment choice had been made.

This employee ended up being replaced by another person, but the work processes have been reorganised so that a recurrence of these problems will not happen; members of staff are now to follow up orders once they have been taken. The supervisor negotiates with the factory for a suitable delivery date and the merchandisers help with the other details.

When the customer contacts the supervisor to discuss the order, the factory is then asked to negotiate with the customer on the suitable delivery date. The merchandisers assist with the details such as the list of products purchased, the schedule and any other order details. No high level of responsibility is then given to the merchandisers, as many of them are not prepared to carry out the duties this would require. This of course poses problems in itself. Should the employees be forced to take responsibility for the duties for which they are paid? Is sufficient training given to these employees? Do they have the capabilities to do the tasks required? They are also not responsible for quality control from the factory, as previously occurred. Finally, no follow-up action is taken with the customers by the merchandiser. This role was passed on to the supervisors and customer service department, thus increasing their workload.

Supply problems

Following the intervention of the manager, work continued for a number of weeks until problems started to escalate again. A problem arose within the factory in that it could not keep the supply of orders up to the level required to meet customer demands. Even though the factory was told that the customers had been promised their goods based on information given by the factory, it was still unable to supply the goods that had been promised.

The manager and the supervisor then had to consult to try to find a solution to this lack of supply. The first issue was to go to the factory to determine what the problems were. Several questions were determined. Was the material ready? Was material available to manufacture the goods? How many workers were involved in manufacturing the required goods? The number of items that could be manufactured on a daily basis was another issue. Other matters, such as how many hours the employees could work, were also discussed, and other consultations were taken to determine if there was an alternative or hidden reason as to why the factory could not deliver the goods as scheduled, and how best to remedy that problem.

Although it was beyond the requirements of the supervisor to do this work, as it was considered that it was the factory's responsibility to supply as promised, because of the backlog in customer orders the supervisor had to go and make personal representation to the factory to determine the reasons for the hold-up. The supervisor considered that it was a special situation as the factory had promised delivery to the supply company, which in turn had promised delivery to the customers.

Discussions then were held with the labouring staff within the factory to determine the real reason. Was the material to manufacture the goods ready? Were the processes that were being used within the factory appropriate? It was decided that there were insufficient people employed by the factory to fill the orders.

The process within the factory was as follows. The first step was to ensure material was available. The major issue concerned the metal tubes required for the framework of the furniture. The second step was to cut the tubes into the required shape and to bend them appropriately. The third step was welding the different materials into the required shape and format. The fourth step was firing the metal tubes. This was required to assist in the powder coating to be placed on the metal. The final step was weaving the rattan onto the furniture framework. The last step on completion of the furniture was the packing of the material or the completed furniture into containers for shipment.

For the weaving process itself the factory needed approximately 200 people. They only had 100 employees available to do this work, therefore the timeframe was extended by a couple of days to complete the finished furniture product. Discussion was then held with the factory owner on the need to hire more people to increase production. Also, packing would take three to four days due to the small number of people that were employed to do this job.

Unfortunately when the supervisory staff were absent from the factory floor many of the employees slackened or reduced their workload, so the supervisors had to stay within the factory to ensure that work met the required schedule. The merchandisers from the factory outlet considered that it was not their work; they were merchandisers, not supervisors. They considered that this work was not their responsibility.

Management then realised that they had to hire a suitable person to ensure that the factory worked at full capacity. It was realised that this person was needed to ensure that the factory maintained its targeted output. Management realised that they required more supervisory staff and production staff to be hired and trained to effectively do the duties required. This was a difficult decision to make, as many of the supervisors viewed it as not their responsibility within the organisation to closely supervise staff as they had too many additional duties that they needed to undertake. This situation was aggravated by staff departures due to the pressure placed on them by the need to hire and train more people, which added to the cost of running the factory and the organisation generally.

Recruitment of staff

In hiring people, the supervisors tended to concentrate on the personality of the individual being hired, not specifically on their identified skills and ability. Although skills and abilities were considered to be significant, the personality and fit of the employee into the organisation were considered very important issues to follow up on. Interviewees were asked questions in a problem-based format about what they would do if a certain predicament arose. Many answered that they would further push the factory if it was not producing and if no satisfactory response was provided, they would then push their manager to see what he could do to encourage the factory to maintain its production rate. A number of people considered that their role might be to stay at the factory to ensure that the correct work was undertaken by staff within a suitable time frame.

It was considered then that many of the new employees, if they were selected and trained adequately, and were given specific instructions, should be told not to consider what is or is not possible but actually to do the work required of them. This would include work that is over and above their normal duties. In other words, higher level employees who displayed initiative in their previous work, and who would carry this initiative on to their current employment, were chosen. It was suggested to the employees that they could actually change their thinking processes to fit in with the international needs of the growing company. It was emphasised that they should look at and analyse the situation and improve both the work needs and themselves continually. In other words, a continual improvement process was promoted within the factory.

Alternative supplier and delivery problems

A problem arose within the organisation, to do with the pricing structure of the furniture provided. Recently, a new factory was approached in which an order was placed for the manufacture of furniture. Before the order was placed with the factory, a suitable price was negotiated between the manufacturer and the wholesaler. The furniture was then promised at a certain price and the contract was appropriately signed. After a number of orders were taken from the customers, the factory wished to raise the price of production to the wholesaler. Unfortunately, the company had no choice, due to the customer orders that had been taken, but to actually pay the price requested by the factory. However the long-term result was that the factory lost any further orders given to them by the company. The company looked for other factories to manufacture its furniture.

During this problematic time with the supplying factory, in which prices were increased, another problem arose. The merchandiser who was in charge of this order resigned from the company. The supervisor was then asked to take over the handling of this order until a new merchandiser could be employed. Before the employee left, she was asked to sum up the main tasks that had to be carried out for the order to be completed, and she stated that she would do this.

After the employee had resigned and left the company, the first new container came out, but no information had been given to forward this container on to the appropriate receiver. In other words, insufficient details were provided to allow the order to be despatched and completed. The role, therefore, was handed to the supervisor to manage. This supervisor, however, would not take responsibility for the order. He needed to ensure that the instructions were correct and to contact the customer to confirm whether the delivery date was satisfactory. Although a number of the duties of the ex-employee had been taken over by the supervisor, he considered that the shipping of the container was not his responsibility.

After discussion with the factory, it was decided that a better way had to be found to ensure that both customers and the organisation were not disadvantaged due to staff resignation and the on-going problem of other staff members' refusal to take responsibility.

Another problem occurred when a new factory started manufacture for the company and promised that it would take over much of the organisation required to ensure the correct goods were placed in the correct shipping container. Unfortunately, this did not work out as the factory made a number of errors, including making the wrong furniture, supplying the wrong colours, and mixing up the orders.

In China even if a contract is signed, a deal may not necessarily hold. This is one of the reasons why various companies do not take responsibility for the work that they have been contracted to do. The main issue, therefore, is relationships and how to maintain those relationships to ensure that a happy supplier–wholesaler–retailer–customer nexus can be provided, in which all parties are happy and the relationship will build as a result. Another issue is how problems can be resolved, such as the choice of material or design being different from what was originally requested by the customer.

It is realised that many factories are not good performers when supplying manufactured goods to wholesalers and retailers. Therefore, the solution is to find good factories and build a strong relationship with them so that problems and difficulties can be analysed, discussed and resolved to the satisfaction of all people. This requires good relationships being built between managers, supervisors and workers at all levels. Factories have to realise that wholesalers and retailers are their customers, to whom they have to provide good customer service by building up a satisfactory relationship.

Organisations have to trust that their employees take responsibility for their duties; employees need to know how to organise the work that is within their direct control. Management must realise what employees can and cannot do, and then refine their processes accordingly to ensure that the correct work is done by capable and responsible people. Employers must find out what the capabilities of the employee are, and give them the work that they can do, passing work that they can't do to other people who are more capable. The alternative is to train employees who don't already have certain capabilities in order to see if they are willing to accept the additional responsibility which the training should prepare them for.

Conclusion

As can be seen above, if effective and valid recruitment measures were in place, many of the problems that arose out of choosing staff that did not fit in with the needs and culture of the company could have been eliminated. Also, appropriate training should be given to allow non-qualified but suitable employees to take up higher positions. Other issues, such as remuneration, benefits, and effective performance, combined with a re-design of certain aspects of the workflow should also be considered.

Problems with supplying companies are another issue that needs attention. It should not be the role of the exporting organisation to supervise the factory staff subcontracted to them to supply goods by a certain date. This aspect needs a tighter control of contract management, in which the expatriate manager needs to have a major role.

References

Deng Xianyong (2006) 'The 3Q recruitment model', *Human Resource Development of China*, 6: 76–78.

Fan Hong and Dai Liangtie (2004) 'A recruitment model based on person–organization fit', *Economic Management*, 3: 68–71.

Fan Hong (2007) 'The trinitarian recruitment model', *Human Resource Development of China*, 2: 58–60.

Huang Yuanming (2006) 'Use three fit recruiting to select the most suitable candidate', *Human Resource Development of China*, 1: 39–42.

Li Zhi and Wang Lin (2006) 'Analysis on the recruitment of the Fortune 500 enterprises', *Human Resource Development of China*, 12: 91–94.

Luo Ming, Xuan Guoliang and Wan Jing (2009) 'Optimizing recruiting strategies with fit philosophy', *Human Resource Development of China*, 2: 25–27.

Peng Yifeng and Huangpu Meifeng (2007) 'Identifying personal integrity in recruiting process', *Human Resource Development of China*, 6: 45–47.

Sun Lin (2009) 'Corporation- and position-based recruiting', *Human Resource Development of China*, 2: 22–24.

Wang Bingcheng and Wang Xianqing (2006) 'On corporate reasons to invalid recruitment', *Human Resource Development of China*, 3: 40–42.

Wang Lanyun (2009) 'Establishment and promotion of effective enterprise recruitment', *Human Resource Development of China*, 2: 34–36.

Human resource problems at the US Vehicles motor factory in central China

Introduction

In certain areas of China, particularly the central and western provinces, the government is trying to encourage new industries to commence operations in an attempt to provide employment, improve living standards, bring new technologies to the region, and provide training to many employees, as well as increase opportunities in general due to flow-on effects. It is considered that this will assist in the further development of many of these areas. This chapter examines the co-ownership of an automobile manufacturing company, located in central China, with partnership jointly shared by Chinese and overseas interests.

This case study covers a range of human resource issues. The major issues affecting the organisation are staff development and cross-cultural aspects existing within the company. Recruitment and remuneration are also discussed, as well as performance management of employees and its link to rewards for staff members. Although there are a number of problems, the organisation, with support from the various stakeholders, is gradually resolving them.

Literature review

Training is an important aspect of any organisation. Its role is not only to increase the skills within the workforce (especially important when new staff are commencing work), but also to realise that the members of the workforce do have many skills that they bring with them into the organisation, which effective training will improve (Denby, 2010). An empirical study from Qin et al. (2007) revealed that training was related to positive company performance and can also moderate the innovation strategy of the organisation and generally be beneficial to business in many ways. This can work towards its role as an agent of change, encouraging staff to be more accepting of many things.

Yao and Chen (2009) proposed the establishment of a training system based on the competency model, which included identifying training needs, designing a training plan, and evaluating training performance. This can be conducted on three levels: evaluation of training courses, post-training examination, and post-training organisational performance to determine the effectiveness of the training.

Li and Shi (2009) mentioned a number of steps to identify training needs through the application of a competency model. These were specifying organisational core competencies, establishing a competency model for specific individual positions, analysing the gap between existing staff competencies and the position-required competency, and designing an appropriate training programme to fill that gap.

Xiang and Li (2004) conducted a survey among staff in private enterprises on their attitudes towards the need for training and found that the top five skills ranked by participants as being essential were managerial skills, work-related knowledge, management concepts, professional skills and sales techniques.

As to the training approach, Mei (2008) suggested corporate coaching as an efficient way to develop staff potential and to provide potential promotional opportunities to employees. Qin and Zhang (2009) proposed the application of case-based reasoning to suit the different training needs of a heterogeneous workforce. Mei (2009) proposed the evaluation of training outcomes through behaviour benchmarking and suggested that both the training department and the functional department be held responsible for evaluating the effects of the training provided to each of the employees.

Training can also be beneficial in the integration of a diverse workforce. With the increasing development of cross-cultural workplaces, due to the need to bring in a larger number of staff with expertise in a particular area to overcome the shortcomings of either an industry or a particular geographic region, individuals from a wider range of racial and ethnic backgrounds will be working together. Traditional methods of resolving potential conflict may not be effective in this environment. There could be an inherent distrust between people of different races, a misunderstanding of institutional values, and the basic communication issues, all leading to cross-cultural conflict (Appelbaum, et al., 1998). The difference in collective versus individual cultures also poses problems, with the potential to lead to conflict (Hofstede, 1980).

Liu and Jing (2006) proposed, through a case study, that cultural conflicts in joint ventures in China existed in the value system (individualism versus collectivism), the thinking patterns (intuitive versus logical), and interpersonal relations (people-oriented versus task-oriented). Wu and Xu (2009) summarised the causes of cultural conflicts in international enterprises as being communication and language issues, religion and customs, and a rigid and inflexible culture. Xie (2008) added conflicting management style to this list.

Jia and Zhu (2006) analysed the root causes of cultural conflict in international companies in China from the view of Chinese traditional culture, and compared Confucianism with Western management theory. Chinese culture places an emphasis on social harmony, while Western culture thinks highly of individual development. Western views of the individual tend to be more practical and utilitarian than that of Confucianism. More value is attached to harmony between man and nature in Confucianism, while Westerners takes a more active view towards the individual influence of the person. Confucianism tends to place a greater emphasis on ruling by morality rather than by law.

Xie (2008) discussed the negative impact of cultural conflict, including damage to work relations, loss of market opportunities and efficiency, and a failure to implement global strategy. The negative opportunities that could result from this, for any organisation, would have a major impact on its viability in the marketplace.

Gu et al. (2003) revealed that the cultural conflicts in multinational corporations (MNCs) in China were reflected in five aspects: namely, inappropriate managerial systems, the behaviour of expatriate managers, lack of cultural respect, no or poor staff development and power–distance relationships. In addition, they found that employees with tenure of five to six years were most likely to sense the conflicts in managerial systems. Moreover, employees in their first or second years in the company feel most dissatisfied in their personal development and will feel increasingly disgruntled after a few years if there is a lack of opportunities for further development.

He and Zhou (2008) put forward an evaluation system of cross-cultural management for MNCs in China. This system evaluates the efficiency of cross-cultural management from four perspectives. These perspectives are the conflicts in the value system and other managerial systems, corporate social responsibility, conflicts between employees with different cultural backgrounds, and innovation in cross-cultural management.

Jiang (2004) considered a number of ways to resolve cross-cultural conflict. These included cultivating cultural awareness, enhancing cultural acceptance, considering cross-cultural factors in human resource planning, giving priority to selecting and promoting people with cross-cultural background, placing an emphasis on socialisation and training in cross-cultural adaptation, constructing differentiated performance management systems, and building a cooperative culture within the company. Similar views were suggested by Liu and Jing (2006), who recommended cross-cultural training on languages, cultural awareness, communication and conflict-handling to solve problems.

The organisation

US Vehicles is a multinational enterprise (MNE), having its main headquarters in the United States, but with subsidiaries in many parts of the world, including China. In China, automobile companies are allowed to set up multinational operations with the provision that there is a substantial Chinese interest in the company. Therefore, all such organisations in China are to be owned on a 50–50 basis; 50 per cent to be owned by the multinational enterprise and the other 50 per cent to be owned by Chinese interests. In this way, China maintains some substantial control over the operations and management of the company.

The first multinational enterprise manufacturing motor cars in China was Chinese Volkswagen, based in Shanghai. Since starting up in 1984 this company has grown to be one of the most successful manufacturers of vehicles in China. Other car companies have followed this lead, setting up their own joint ventures to capitalise on one of the fastest growing vehicle markets in the world. In China, the Chinese US Vehicles Motor Company (CVMC) is a joint venture operation between US Vehicles and its Chinese partners, which commenced in 2001. In 2005, a decision was made to change the existing shareholding structures. Originally, the company was 50 per cent owned by US Vehicles and 50 per cent owned by a Shanghai-based organisation. The Shanghai component was run by a government-owned subsidiary, which at the time provided machinery and other associated equipment to government institutions. Currently, however, ownership of the Chinese operation is divided between the controlling company (15 per cent), US Vehicles

(15 per cent), and CVMC (20 per cent), with the remaining 50 per cent owned by the China Group.

It must be noted that the controlling company is owned by US Vehicles. US Vehicles has two Chinese plants, both located in central China. The approach to joint ventures between Western countries and China tends to be very different from that existing in other countries. The cultural barrier between the two partners is the major concern for each of them in reaching an agreement about how the organisation will be managed, both on a daily operational basis and extending to long-term strategies that will assist the company to further expand into the Chinese market. These barriers have the potential to impact on the long-term decision-making ability of the company if there is a clash of opinion between the joint owners.

The main manufacturing plant produces a number of different makes of vehicle for the domestic market, and employs in excess of 5,000 people. The plant is fully unionised, with union members being part of an enterprise union, and belonging to Changan US Vehicles Joint Automobile Company Union. The employees union tends to ensure that good working conditions are maintained, in close liaison with the management of the operation. To confirm this view, a review of recent press and media reports and releases regarding human rights issues at the plant did not reveal any issues of concern.

The partner plant is responsible for the manufacturing of vehicle components, as well as having responsibility for parts assembly and other miscellaneous manufacturing activities. At the main plant, the cars are fully assembled, using the components from the partner. The completed range includes the US Vehicles 'Future' model, the popular 'Commuter' model, and other less popular specialist models.

The service organisation of the company is also located in the main facility. This part of the organisation provides customer support to the various distributors located around China, as well as assisting dealers in their promotions and various marketing campaigns. Support is provided in line with the motto of the parent company: 'one US Vehicles, one plant, one goal'. The rationale behind this motto is to reduce costs, share resources, and try to inculcate in the employees, distributors and salespeople those same values. The brand needs to be rebuilt and the culture of the organisation also needs to be changed to focus on this goal. In support of the parent company motto, the slogan of the Chinese organisation is 'make every day exciting'. This is to be a challenge to all employees to strive for perfection and to be innovative.

The problems

The main problem at CVMC is to do with restrictions on the development of the organisation and its people. In the local company headquarters this centres on recruitment of qualified people due to financial restrictions on paying higher salaries to attract new employees at all levels and to retain those experienced and trained staff members currently working in the plant. A shortage of qualified staff is also of concern, not only in this particular facility, but also in other areas of the country.

One of the reasons the best qualified people cannot be recruited into the company is that the organisation is restricted from offering the most competitive package to get the most suitable employees. This extends from the recruiting of line managers down to the base level manual employees within the plant. Even though the recruiters know that many of the applicants for positions are not qualified to the level required by the company, they still need to recruit them as there is no other source of suitable employees in the vicinity, with the right mix of skills and qualifications. If they were allowed to offer a better compensation package, staff could be poached from other companies or might be tempted to migrate from other provinces, although this could pose a problem in itself with many other provinces being unprepared to let valued staff leave their areas.

To try to alleviate these problems, there was a proposal previously raised that the sales centre should be moved to Shanghai due to the larger availability of qualified staff, coupled with the fact that Shanghai is considered to be the economic centre of China. With better access to suitably qualified staff, whom some managers consider are capable of doing a better job than those located in the current head office, sales would improve. The Chinese partnership, however, rejected the suggestion on two counts. First, if the company (or at least the sales division) remains in the current location, it allows the Chinese owners to make money due to the cheaper cost of labour, facilities and other tax and resource advantages in the province. Second, it brings technology to an area of China in which it is lacking. The introduction of this technology, coupled with appropriate training, works to assist in modernising this part of the country. Social reasons, therefore, are a component of the decisions being made with respect to this industry.

Social factors, however, are not a new concern of the Chinese government or, for that matter, many other governments around the world. Many companies are asked to decentralise to reduce pressure on the infrastructure of larger cities and to increase opportunities for training and employment in remote areas. To encourage this decentralisation, taxation advantages and other benefits may be provided, including the provision of training institutes or universities to ensure that there is a skilled labour supply available.

The training of staff to ensure they have the appropriate skills and knowledge to allow them to operate efficiently and effectively has been another problem at CVMC, especially at the start-up and development phases of the business, as many new staff do not have the skills that are urgently needed and it can be costly to train them up to an appropriate level. The other shortfall is in the general management skills of many of the supervisors, especially in their handling of conflict within the company, which occurs at all levels but is more likely to be disruptive in a major way on the plant operations at the shop-floor level. To some extent, this is a reflection on the mix of employees from various cultural backgrounds.

Therefore, another issue of concern is the cross-cultural aspect of the organisation, which can have both positive and negative connotations. At the management level in the central Chinese plant there is a broad mix of people of different nationalities. There also appears to be some dissension among management ranks as to what strategies should be undertaken due to the different perspectives of staff of different nationalities, coupled with what has worked for them in previous employment. There are a substantial number of conflicts occurring within the organisation, due to these cultural differences. Although it is realised that conflict can be positive, a lack of clear direction from management is not helpful. It needs to be noted that, as the United States partner is a true multinational, it has placed into the management structure staff from many different countries.

So to summarise the major problems, there exists conflict among staff at all levels, a lack of sufficiently trained staff, low levels of compensation, no proper performance criteria and cross-cultural concerns with the expatriates.

Resolution of the problems – conflict management

The company has tried to resolve the conflict problems through the adoption of a compromise approach. This approach was written into the policies of the company after much consultation between senior levels of management and an examination of various dispute resolution procedures used by other organisations.

The first stage in the process is to debate the issues involved between all affected parties, where the different perspectives and areas of concern would be studied. If any aggravated conflict occurs, it generally comes at this stage of the negotiation process. If there appears to be no clear solution, the parties are encouraged to leave to allow them to think over alternatives to the problems.

After this stage the parties resume discussions, and some form of compromise then normally occurs, in which the parties work out a reasonable solution to the problem. An outcome that is satisfactory to all parties is then reached and agreed on. This strategy, however, takes time, during which there can be substantial loss of production. To alleviate this, it is agreed that a representative will negotiate, while the affected parties perform their normal duties. This then results in minimum disruption to the plant.

If considered necessary, a mediator can be invited to assist in resolving the conflict. Although not a preferred solution, it is a final resort if neither party can come to some amicable arrangement.

Training

It became apparent, soon after operations commenced, that people were being hired with insufficient skills to perform the duties required of them. The reason for this is that the region in which the plant is located consists of a lower-skilled pool of talent. However, it is possible that a factor in the Chinese partners choosing to locate the company in central China was to raise the level of skills in that province, and as a result, raise the standard of living over time. Hence there was a need to provide training to staff, as it was considered that increased skills would raise the standard of living not only of the staff undertaking the training, but also of the wider population.

The company therefore needed to devise a training plan, and it was decided that training would commence in 2009. The initial training programme was estimated to last for two years, and begin by focusing on managers and supervisors. The aim was to train the line managers to be more effective in their management of staff, their handling of problems, as well as the numerous financial and budgetary matters, among others.

There was some doubt, though, as to whether the right decisions regarding this programme and the implementation plans for the training had been put into practice. Other skills apart from those mentioned above and that were considered to be required by the line managers were initially omitted, but due to pressure from the partners, other aspects were later incorporated into the programme. These other modules included crisis management, how to chair and manage meetings, how to manage a strong team, and how to be a successful manager. Management finance and marketing were also key attributes that would be provided to the line managers through the programme.

Job specific training also needed to be given. The first phase of the training was to provide these common core areas to all the line managers at the same time. However, this focus on line managers tends to shy away from the low skill levels of the factory staff. No training programme was provided for these employees, although the skills that were needed by many of them were essential for the effective maintenance and operations of the production line.

Compensation and performance

Compensation and employee incentives also needed to be addressed by the organisation. As the salary paid to the employees was below average compared to similar factories, demonstrating external inequity problems, a people development committee was formed to examine and assist management to decide on the overall employment conditions of the staff. As part of its agenda, it was also to incorporate the wage levels of the employees at both management and production levels.

This was to be based to some extent on the performance targets of the management employees and their individual assessments using a 360 degree appraisal method. Although this is potentially an expensive and awkward system to implement over a large number of staff members, the organisation considered that it was the preferred method to gain the best impression of management by all of the affected stakeholders within the company. This not only included the senior management of the company, but the views of other employees were also sought as part of the exercise.

If the performance of the staff member was classed as satisfactory, they would then receive an increase of 10 per cent of their base pay. For more senior management it was possible that they might get up to a 20 per cent per year increase, as long as they were considered to be exceptional performers within the company. An aspect of the performance development assessment that was used on management staff was the US Vehicles International Behaviours Ratings scales. There are a number of ratings for the management within US Vehicles, ranging from below average to superior performance, and the salary increases as a result of the performance of employees can vary significantly. It was planned to bring this same system into operation in the central China plants. Discussion was held as to whether this system should be modified to make it culturally appropriate, but the management decided against adapting the system to suit local needs. The implications of this refusal to make the system culturally appropriate have not been determined.

Cross-cultural conflict

The third issue is cross-cultural conflict. The different parties and nationalities have tended to aggravate decision-making within the company. As the company is a multinational enterprise, it is to be expected that there will be both management and technical staff sent to the Chinese plant for both short and long-term projects, so some conflict could be expected based on the differing personalities and positions of the staff. Whether the conflict is true cross-cultural conflict between the Chinese management and other nationalities, or is more based on the power and politics existing within the plant, between the various levels of authority given to staff at various levels is debatable. This issue closely relates to the expatriate relationships.

Expatriates

The issue of expatriates is of interest and should be noted as to their potential contribution to the company as well as the problems that may occur due to selecting candidates who do not integrate well into the culture. Many of the expatriates come to the Chinese plants on a three year contract. Whether or not the expatriate employees are doing a good job is the decision of the joint venture. The Chinese owners and the US Vehicles owners co-decide on whether to replace expatriate staff with local managers. The matter of localisation is of increasing importance to both the Chinese and American management. The advantages of a localisation policy are that communication between management and staff is easier, it saves money for the venture, and the local managers better understand the culture of the workers. However, if the expatriate managers are doing well, an extension of another three years may be granted to these employees, as the American shareholder wishes to have some control over the direction of the operation.

Conclusion

Even though there may be a number of inefficiencies in the organisation, these have tended to be hidden by the growth in demand for automobiles in China. For example, over a two-year period sales have gone from 100,000 units to over 200,000 units, an effective doubling of sales. The confidence that the company has in the Chinese market, despite a number of problems, is demonstrated by the decision to expand its operation in the country.

A number of problems were highlighted in the study, however, which could impact on operations. The issue of conflict needs to be remedied, and training and better management systems can influence this aspect of the company. The use of a grievance mechanism and mediators, along with consultation and discussion had resulted in minimal industrial dispute despite cultural differences. Aligning remuneration with an employee's performance may seem appropriate, but the cultural differences mentioned above need to be considered to ensure that the system is viewed as fair and equitable to all staff.

Finally, expatriate issues need to be monitored to ensure that suitable staff are employed who are culturally sensitive to the environment. A move to a localisation plan could be viewed in the longer term as a more suitable management method, but in the interim the knowledge, skills and abilities that these staff bring to the area are valuable, and as long as this knowledge is imparted to local staff, these employees should be retained.

References

Appelbaum, S., Shapiro, B. and Elbaz, D. (1998) 'The management of multicultural group conflict', *Team Performance Management*, 4(5): 211–234.

Denby, S. (2010) 'The importance of training needs analysis', *Industrial and Commercial Training*, 42(3): 147–150.

Gu Qingliang et al (2003) 'A study on cultural conflict in MNCs in China', *Journal of Donghua University (Social Sciences)*, 3(1): 6–14.

He Lihong and Zhou Hui (2008) 'On the establishment of evaluation indicator system of cross-cultural management in MNCs in China', *Academic Journal of Zhongzhou*, 5: 59–62.

Hofstede, G. (1980) 'Motivation, leadership, and organizations: do American theories apply abroad?', *Organizational Dynamics*, 9(1): 42–63.

Jia Xiaoyan and Zhu Yongxin (2006) 'Management of cross-cultural shock in MNCs: on the perspective of Confucianism', *Science of Science and Management of S.&T.*, 6: 126–128.

Jiang Zhaoyi (2004) 'Solutions to the cross-cultural conflict of transnational enterprises', *Journal of China West Normal University (Philosophy and Social Sciences)*, 5: 97–99.

Liu Shumin and Shi Kan (2009) 'Competency-based training needs analysis', *Human Resource Development of China*, 3: 49–51.

Liu Pu and Jing Runtian (2006) 'Case analysis of cross-cultural conflicts between Chinese-foreign joint ventures', *Chinese Journal of Management*, 3(1): 113–116.

Mei Feng (2009) 'Binary evaluation of training outcomes from the perspective of "behavior benchmarking"', *Human Resource Development of China*, 1: 51–53.

Mei Yiwei (2008) 'Coaching – an important training approach for staff development', *Human Resource Development of China*, 5: 20–22.

Qin Xiuaolei, Yang Dongtao and Wei Jiangru (2007) 'An empirical research of the relation of innovation strategy and training with firm performance in manufacturing industry', *Chinese Journal of Management*, 4(3): 354–357.

Qin Yan and Zhang Guoliang (2009) 'The application of case-based reasoning in knowledge-enabled human resource development', *Human Resource Development of China*, 3: 39–42.

Wu Guoying and Xu Li (2009) 'The structure of organization management and coordination mechanism based on the cross-cultural conflict', *Journal of Nanjing University of Finance and Economics*, 2: 68–71.

Xiang Zheng and Li Zhi (2004) 'An empirical study in staff attitude and needs to corporate training in private enterprises', *Sci-Technology and Management*, 6: 129–131.

Xie Shuqing (2008) 'Study on cross-cultural conflict and strategies in MNCs', *Economic Theory and Business Management*, 10: 77–80.

Yao Kai and Chen Man (2009) 'Constructing training systems using competency model', *Chinese Journal of Management*, 6(4): 532–536.

Management and staffing at a start-up regional airlines company

Introduction

The airline industry in China is a fast-growing market, although, as with many airlines around the world, it does have its own financial, regulatory and staffing problems. This chapter examines some of the problems that are being faced by a new regional airline in central China. Issues such as staffing with suitably qualified pilots, training, budget, and the management and organisational structure are examined, as the airline seeks to become a viable concern in the regional market.

The approach adopted by the airline is to develop a niche local market, with assistance and support from both Chinese and overseas partners. Gaining acceptance of the proposed structure by the majority stakeholders has caused some concern among the local management of the airline, with a number of restrictions being imposed on it. Health and safety issues are also a problem, with limits placed by the government on allowable flying times for the pilots. However, the major concern seems to be organisational planning and structure and its related impact on performance, which needs to be finalised by management prior to any longer-term planning taking place.

Literature review

Distribution of power and responsibility is the fundamental content of organisation planning. But due to a lack of theoretical structure, difficulties exist in management practices. Huang (2003) argued that line authority should be assigned to be consistent with responsibilities and personal capabilities, and should be linked to the position holder's own interest in order to lower agency costs. The distribution of line authority may vary, depending on the scale of enterprise, management level, capital abundance, corporate culture and personal competence.

Duan (2007) studied the major factors influencing organisational planning in insurance companies and suggested that corporate strategy, information technology, important stakeholders such as the government, the parent company and major shareholders, and other companies in the industry had a significant impact on the organisational planning of the company. Additionally, organisational planning needs to take the external environment and the nature of the organisation into consideration and find a balance between efficiency and effectiveness in decision-making (Fang and Zhou, 2000). When changes occur in either internal or external environments, organisational strategy and structure must adapt accordingly (Luo, 2008).

Chen and Wang (2007) found that functional structure is the most common structure among private technology companies in China, with the matrix structure least used. Many companies fail to put sufficient emphasis on organisation planning, resulting in inconsistency in their organisational structures and companies' development stage and developmental pattern.

Zhu and Wang (2009) studied the relationship between organisational structure and performance in Chinese enterprises and found that the more uncertain the environment was, the less formal the structure was and the more liaison mechanisms the company needed in order to ensure its performance. The larger the enterprise is, the more significant these correlations tend to be. To the smaller enterprises, environment has a greater direct and significant impact on performance.

An opposite opinion exists between the relationship of an enterprise's structural inertia and corporate performance. From the perspective of a resource-based view, structural inertia means good performance. From the contrary perspective, inertia theory gets an opposite conclusion. Liu et al. (2009) suggested that it was necessary for Chinese enterprises to possess inertia to some extent. However, if the inertia is very strong, blocking their development, strategic change should be carried out to motivate the enterprises. On the other hand, at the time of an enterprise's inception or when it is faced with bankruptcy, aggressive and frequent strategic change will destroy its stability and negatively affect its performance.

Zhang et al. (2009) proposed that the more organic the organisational structure was, the more motivated the organisation members tended to be in knowledge transfer, the more rapidly they improved their capability of knowledge transfer and the more diversified the knowledge transfer channels were, all leading to the enhancement of technological innovation capacity in the organisation.

Compared to traditional hierarchical structures, companies with a strong service philosophy are very different: employee relations are like those between service-provider and customers, instead of superior and subordinates; employees are driven by the demands of the internal supply chain rather than managers. Therefore, the structural design of a service organisation should move from sales (who face customers directly) to its supporting functions in the internal supply chain and from the implementation department to management (Xiao and Liu, 2009).

The organisation

Regional Airlines is an airline company in China which is engaged in the transportation of both passengers and goods. It is a relatively new regional airline company and was established in early 2007. Its first flight was later that year. It is currently based in a town in the central-northern region of China, and it is a joint venture with one of the biggest airline companies in China, which has a 50 per cent ownership stake. Another partner is an American-based airline company. It owns 49 per cent of the shares of Regional Airlines.

The company currently has over 180 employees. Although only a small airline, it has plans to expand into the wider Chinese market. Its aim is to be a low-cost regional airline, servicing many smaller cities that are not adequately serviced by the larger airline companies. Most of Regional Airlines' flights take an average of 40 minutes, with a small number extending to 100 minutes. Generally, however, it is only a short flight, short distance commuter airline company. In 2008 the airline moved to another location in China. The reasons for this move were to take advantage of a larger labour market with better support facilities.

The airline currently has 15 aircraft; the goal is to have 50 aircraft in operation by the end of 2011, with the prime aim being to become the largest regional airline in China.

The employees

Employees consist of both ground staff and crew members. Most of the staff have transferred from a partner airline in China with the exception of a small number of the pilots and flight attendants. There are also several foreign captains who were recruited from the United States.

In the management team there are currently 18 staff employed. There is a general manager of engineering, who is responsible for the maintenance and engineering staff and facilities, and there is a general manager of operations, who is responsible for the operational aspects of the airline. The senior management team consists of a general manager and chief financial officer, who are both appointees from the Chinese partner.

The airline has six departments.

- Safety and regulations, which is of major importance to the airline, is responsible for ensuring that the airline operates under the safety guidelines set by the Chinese authorities.

- Flight operations is responsible for despatching and ensures that crew are rostered on to operate the planes, and that passengers and freight are loaded.

- Maintenance and engineering certifies the fitness of the aircraft to fly, as well as undertaking regular scheduled maintenance of the fleet, and other repairs as needed.

- Marketing and sales is responsible for promoting the airline and issuing tickets, as well as increasing the freight orders to ensure that the flights are fully loaded.

- Administration looks after general administration issues. (Human Resources is included in this department.)

- Planning and financial services focuses on the long-term growth of the company and monitors income, cash-flow and finance.

The problems

By the the middle of 2008 the airline had already opened over 50 domestic routes. One of the problems encountered, however, was a shortage of pilots. This was a problem that was not unique to this airline, but was quite widespread across China. The implications were that the pilots were working an increased number of hours in order to service the available airline routes. It also affected the ability of the airline to expand further in the domestic market.

The lack of a suitable organisational structure at the moment is another of the major problems facing the airline. As their Chinese airline partner is the major stakeholder, many of the functions of Regional Airlines are currently carried out by this operator. The goal of the partner airline is to make money using a built-in management model. From the initial organisation chart, it can be noted that many of the support functions are done by the partner. Functions such as the marketing department, network planning and the ticketing system use the partner's systems. The advantage of this is that it saves money through the sharing of resources with the partner airline.

Pilot training is one of the issues that is also managed by the partner. It is crucial for the safety aspects and licensing of the airline to have qualified staff. The use of joint functions from the partner airline has allowed Regional Airlines to expand beyond what it would normally be able to do without this assistance. It has also allowed an earlier approval from the Civil Aviation Administration of China (CAAC) for Regional Airlines to operate than would normally be the case.

There are, however, a number of problems arising from the sharing of the facilities. One of the main issues of contention is the imposition of the policies of the partner airline onto Regional Airlines. The partner has over 8,000 staff and the imposition of these policies, which are really based on a large airline, onto a small airline having only 180 staff tends not to be a comfortable fit. Communication between the two airlines is also a major problem. As an example, a plane was ready to take off but it was found that there were no passengers waiting to board the flight. It turned out that the partner had forgotten to update their system and had not marketed or advertised this flight. So a flight was ready to fly with full crew but with no passengers. The end result was that the flight had to be cancelled, with a substantial loss of money for a small company. Costs included crewing costs and airport taxes, as well as cost of fuel to fly to the next destination for the next leg of the flight. This added an unexpected and unnecessary cost to the start-up company, which was not reimbursed by the partner.

Another issue lies with the organisational structure of Regional Airlines. Their organisational chart may have a number of people or positions missing because a particular function is shared with the partner airline. Unfortunately when the CAAC inspects the organisational structure, if they find a number of gaps in the organisation, there is a possibility that they could cancel the licence of the fledgling airline, even though the roles are jointly shared with a larger partner. Because of this possibility, the general manager has to consider filling the full organisational staff complement, even though this increases the costs to the company.

The role that was given to the human resources department, therefore, was to write policies specific to Regional Airlines and also to devise a suitable organisational structure based on CAAC requirements. To create this organisational structure, Regional Airlines had to refer to its American partner airline, other regional airlines in China, and its Chinese partner. To resolve the problem, HR consulted with the manager of each department within the organisation to determine what job positions they considered were necessary to efficiently and safely run the airline. Also the number of levels required within each department had to be confirmed. The problem, of course, was that each manager wanted more staff employed than the airline had the capacity to pay for. The end result was an organisational chart which was too big for the airline to operate efficiently. This chart then had to be handed in to the vice-president of the organisation for his review and possible approval or modification of the proposed structure.

An example of the possible cost blow-out coupled with the staffing and organisational needs of the departments was that the engineering department wished to purchase expensive equipment, which it considered necessary for effective maintenance of the aircraft. Although the function for which this equipment and operating staff were required could be potentially outsourced to another company, the stipulation in the CAAC standards was that the airline itself needed to have this equipment.

The final proposed organisational structure was then handed to the HR department of the Chinese partner airline. The reason for this was that, as the parent company, the partner had the final say in approving for the organisational structure. One of the ironies was that the vice-president of the partner was also the general manager of Regional Airlines, and his role was to balance priorities and roles and to provide communication between the two companies.

The HR department of the partner airline did not like the new structure and as a result cut many positions. This did not sit well with Regional Airlines management, as it demonstrated their lack of autonomy in managing their own affairs.

Another problem was in the flight planning department. This department is responsible for crew resources but not for obtaining the crew to fly particular planes on particular days. The American partner advised them that this function was the responsibility of the despatching department. However, in China it is very difficult to communicate with pilots as to the reporting structure. Pilots tend to have the upper hand due to their extreme shortage, not only in China but worldwide. It is quite common for pilots to refuse to fly certain flights for various reasons. However, the captains can communicate with the pilots, due to the hierarchical system of operation and control within most airlines. This is the reason why most Chinese airlines put the function of crewing a plane into the flight department's area of responsibility, not into the domain of the despatching department.

Finally after much negotiation and re-organisation, the organisational chart was completed and approved by the HR department of the partner airline. It was then handed to the general manager of Regional Airlines for his final approval. Unfortunately, he did not give any feedback to HR as to the success, acceptance or otherwise of the organisational chart. However, the company did not have sufficient money to implement the new organisational structure fully anyway and was required to outsource a number of the functions, although even this could not be done to the extent needed. The problem was how to ensure a high quality of service and product from the outsourcing organisation, as well as to pay them. Another issue was that the CAAC required these functions to be carried out in-house. This posed a quandary for the company.

The existing staff ended up having to work longer hours to cover the shortages, but unfortunately this still led to delays in completion of certain services. The result was that more staff needed to be employed to complete the functions in-house. Training time with the colleges that were supplying these staff was four to five years, meaning the airline, which had only been in existence for one year, had a long wait before staff were sufficiently trained and capable to take over the functions.

Any staff that were recruited from the colleges straight away would need to go into a number of areas, including pilots, engineers and other maintenance staff. The company would also be responsible for obtaining the licences of these new employees, and the training costs of the new recruits could be quite substantial. Also, due to insufficient facilities in certain parts of China a number of the staff may have to be sent overseas for their training.

It was decided that, to fit the organisational structure, approximately 150 college students needed to be recruited. One issue was how to get the money to pay and train these college students. Another problem was how to retain them within the organisation once they had been trained, due to the extreme shortage of people with the needed skills, and the better money that larger companies would be prepared to pay for these highly skilled workers.

The solution

The solution to this dilemma was to have the staff sign a training agreement. A bond system was set up whereby if the staff left they had to refund part of the training costs to the organisation on a pro-rata basis. For example, if the training agreement was for two years and an employee left the company after one year, that employee had to refund half of the cost of training. Unfortunately (and probably understandably), many employees were reluctant to bond themselves to the airline for a set period of time, as they wished to maintain their flexibility to leave if a better position was offered elsewhere. The problem then was whether to train staff and have the airline cover the cost in the hope that the staff would then feel some obligation towards the company for the opportunities given to them, or whether to have untrained staff work under close supervision, but who also would not be as productive to the company. There are obviously both positive and negative aspects of each.

The airline finally decided to cover the cost of the training. An agreement was put in place where financial assistance was given for staff training, in the hope that the staff would remain for a reasonable period of time. However, even though they had the training agreement some of the newly recruited personnel still left and went to work for other larger airlines after the completion of their training course. The airline then had to look at other ways of obtaining qualified staff to ensure levels were acceptable.

College recruitment appeared to be the most successful way of getting qualified employees to work for the organisation, and the HR department visited quite a large number of colleges to recruit staff into the new airline. In 2009 it was planned to send many of the trainees overseas to receive additional training. As an example, staff who were going to work on newly-purchased Brazilian planes would need to be sent to Brazil to learn the maintenance functions of this airline. Although the company offered free training to the Chinese employees, it was still a cost to the airline to actually send these staff overseas due to airfares, immigration requirements, accommodation and other expenses that would be incurred. The agreement, then, was made that these employees, once they were sent overseas, had to work at the airline for three, four or five years depending on the cost of their training. The incentive of overseas travel assisted the airline in gaining a number of college students to agree to the programme.

The structure

Although the organisational structure was finally passed after substantial negotiation and modification, many managers from the different departments complained that they still had insufficient staff to undertake the functions required of them. The managers wished to know how many staff they could employ, but they did not necessarily have the budget to pay for the cost of the new staff. The costing of the new positions required was also very difficult. All of the managers wanted to know how many staff they could employ, and if the cost exceeded the budget given, approval was required for the extra funds. Additionally, for each new employment request, approval needed to be sought from the general manager by the HR department, to ensure that funds were available to recruit these new employees. It turned out to be a very complicated and long process to obtain this approval, due to the tight financial situation of the airline.

A further problem with the staffing structure was the issue of the 'borrowed' staff. Even though many staff transferred from the Chinese partner airline to the new company at the start-up of the business, they were still covered by the labour agreement of the partner airline's industrial agreement. They still considered themselves to be employees of this airline, and not Regional Airlines employees. This resulted in mixed loyalty among the employees. Although the argument was that, when the employees transferred to Regional Airlines, the labour agreement should be cancelled, many of the employees preferred to maintain their contract with the previous company. The general manager, therefore, decided to allow the employees to keep their industrial relationship with the partner. The employees considered that the partner airline was more secure and stable and they could return to their former position if problems arose with Regional Airlines.

Many of the employees who had transferred from the partner airline to Regional Airlines considered that they were only there on a temporary basis, even though the reality was that they could be there for the long term. The view, of course, was that many of the workers, although they were working for Regional Airlines, still had mixed loyalties as mentioned earlier. The view of the human resources department was that if the employees were working for Regional Airlines, then they were employees of Regional Airlines, not of the partner. However, if the labour agreement was transferred and the employees signed a Regional Airlines labour agreement the reality was that many of the employees might have returned to the other company, which would have left Regional Airlines even more short-staffed. Loyalty, therefore, tended to be non-existent among these employees, but there was little that the smaller company could do, based on their urgent need for qualified staff.

Additionally, even though the fledgling airline continued to import new aircraft, they had insufficient pilots and insufficient engineering staff to maintain services. Although they flew to a number of airports, they did not have ground staff in those airports to maintain the planes. Customer services also tended to be non-existent in many of the airports to which they flew. Airline service quality, therefore, could not be guaranteed.

To get back to the key problem, however, the organisational structure still was not finalised and approved by senior management within the organisation. If all managers were familiar with the organisation's chart, it would probably have a pay structure included with it. This chart would then include as an appendix, not only the positions, but also the pay grading and associated salary structure for all staff in each division of the company, effectively giving managers knowledge of their budget for staffing levels.

Although many staff were required, without the approved organisational structure it was difficult to actually recruit, pay and retain them. Also problematic was the requirement that the airline make money as soon as possible, although most start-up airlines normally take four to five years before they start making a profit. Furthermore, one of the major partners was considering leaving the partnership. If this occurred, it would then pose greater financial difficulties for the new airline. Although the United States based partner was lending a number of planes to Regional Airlines, these planes were very old and required a substantial investment in spare parts, maintenance and upkeep. The number of defects that were found on these planes also caused concern, not only to the engineering staff who were responsible for ensuring safety, but also to the pilots who were reluctant to fly the old equipment.

The dumping of aircraft by the US partner into the Chinese market, and their simultaneous criticism of the new airline for its decision to purchase new aircraft in China and Brazil caused problems in the partnership. But the reason that the airline had to purchase these aircraft was that, due to the small number of aircraft that it had on the ground, if an aircraft had a problem, as was very common due to the age of the aircraft that were given to Regional by the US partner airline, the flight had to be cancelled and the passengers had to have their money refunded. This resulted in a bad image for the new company. They were criticised by the US airline for purchasing new aircraft without consulting adequately with them. This seemed contradictory on the part of the partner, who was obviously concerned with maintaining their record in the United States but not with the safety record of the new airline in China.

Conclusion

This case study raises a number of issues to do with starting a new organisation in China and, for that matter, in many other countries as well.

The problems of staffing, training and structure tend to be universal and are well illustrated in this case. Occupational health and safety aspects are also a major cause of concern, for the company, its staff and its potential passengers. Compliance with appropriate regulations is obviously needed, as any breach will reflect negatively on the company, potentially resulting in it losing its licence to operate.

To some extent, it also demonstrates partnership problems, where an established partner in this instance is providing old and defective equipment to the new market. A problem arises when the old equipment requires a high level of maintenance, hence creating a staffing issue, and the new organisation has difficulty in obtaining the staff numbers required for this task. When adequate staff can be employed, there are the related issues of training and retaining them. This is especially problematic in a market in which there is a distinct lack of skilled personnel, resulting in ample opportunity to move to other employment.

References

Chen Kai and Wang Xiaofan (2007) 'Research on organization strucutre of private technology firms in China', *Forum on Science and Technology in China*, 7: 65–67.

Duan Qiuping (2007) 'Organizational planning in insurance companies', *Studies of International Finance*, 7: 66–71.

Fang Weiguo and Zhou Hong (2000) 'Organizational structure design under environment of uncertainty', *Journal of Management Sciences in China*, 3(2): 9–14.

Huang Jinfu (2003) 'Distribution of power and responsibility in designing organization', *Management Review*, 15(8): 59–62.

Liu Haijian, Zhou Xiaohu and Long Jing (2009) 'Organization structural inertia, strategic change and firm performance: an approach of dynamic evolutionary theory', *Management Review*, 21(11): 92–100.

Luo Min (2008) 'Organization design: strategic choice, organizational structure and institutions', *Contemporary Economy and Management*, 30(5): 1–8.

Xiao Yong and Liu Weihua (2009) 'Service philosophy based organizational design', *Human Resource Management of China*, 1: 43–46.

Zhang Guanglei, Zhou Herong and Liao Jianqiao (2009) 'Effects of cooperative organizational structures on the technical innovation from the perspective of the knowledge transferring – a new theory framework', *Science of Science and Management of S&T*, 8: 78–84.

Zhu Xiaowu and Wang Ling (2009) 'Empirical study on the relationship between Chinese enterprise organizational structure and performance in transition period', *Economic Management Journal*, 31(5): 140–146.

Human resource problems during a merger and acquisition

Introduction

This chapter examines a merger and acquisition exercise between two multinational enterprises (MNEs) with head offices in the United States, but with substantial operations in Asia. The take-over demonstrates the differing culture and management styles within the organisations and the problems that both face and have had to deal with. The case study is of Electronic Research Organisation, which was being taken over by Network Systems.

As with any mergers (or acquisitions), there are a number of human resource issues that can have an impact on the success or otherwise of the integration. This is possibly due to the fear that employees may have about the changes and how they will affect them. If dealt with effectively and sympathetically, the morale and motivation of staff should be maintained. If not, staff may resign, leaving a major skills gap within the company. This study deals with a number of matters following a less-than-successful merger and acquisition in the view of the acquired company, including training and staff reduction as a result of the take-over, and also provides an interesting view of staff recruitment, in which the 'best' potential employee is not necessarily the best choice. Issues of leadership style, expatriate leadership and industrial matters, including the change in approach to employment law in China, are also discussed in this chapter.

Literature review

The success rate of mergers and acquisitions among Chinese enterprises is considered to be very low in the sense of long-term performance

(Huang and Linghu, 2005). Summarizing the reasons for the causes of the failure of acquisitions, Huang and Linghu considered that there were two categories, namely, governmental and corporate. They conjectured that incompatible corporate culture between the acquiring and acquired companies makes the post-acquisition integration more difficult, thus hindering the value creation capability of the newly created company. Further studies identified poor post-acquisition integration risk as one of the major issues involved in the merger and aquisition process, including risks to human resource integration, to cultural integration and to organisation and management system integration, all posing threats to the performance of the new company, causing loss of key staff, and failure in the transfer and creation of core competencies (Tang and Feng, 2007).

In fact, Chinese researchers have long been thinking that integration of corporate culture and human resources play a vital role in the success rate of corporate acquisitions (Liao and Li, 2003; Huang and Linghu, 2005; Wu and Chen, 2006; Yan and Wang, 2007; Tang and Feng, 2007; Tang, 2007), while differences in corporate culture impose a potential barrier to the cultural integration between the merging companies (Liao and Li, 2003). Differences in the HR management system, changes in role requirements, threats to personal power and position and changes in team members are identified as causes of conflicts during acquisition. Such cultural conflicts will possibly hinder the new company's capacity in institutional, managerial, technological and cultural innovation (Ma et al., 2009).

Therefore, it is necessary for the human resources department to evaluate the culture and HR practices in the target company, including salary level, benefits, the performance appraisal system, and industrial relations before any acquiring decisions are made (Tang, 2007), since the synergy effect in the corporate culture is the driving force in cultural integration in the new organisation (Liao and Li, 2003). Additionally, the HR department may need to consider the existing senior management style in the acquired company, as well as the retention, training and further development of the employees, the managerial system and procedures, the culture system, and executive pay, as they are all key factors that will affect post-acquisition integration (Sun and Wu, 2009).

Some Chinese companies have already realised the importance of cultural integration. Peng (2008) studied the acquisition conducted by China Southern Airline. Being the first state-owned enterprise (SOE) in China to conduct a cultural audit during an acquisition process, it conducted in-depth interviews with the middle and senior management of the companies involved in the acquisition to explore the potential cultural differences between these companies. Questionnaires were designed to be distributed among employees to better understand the true culture in the companies and these were used to determine concrete measures to address any problems.

The contribution of human resource integration in corporate acquisitions can be summarised into the control of the acquisition cost and the contribution to the value creation after acquisition. The HR department needs to have in place a detailed plan on human resource integration, including characteristics of the human resources in the two companies, its organisational structure, vacancies and overlapping positions in the new company, and a new HR strategy (for recruiting, selecting and performance management among other concerns) based on the aims and projections of the new company (Peng, 2004). Li and Wei (2008) also proposed that the integration of established interest may be the core of human resource integration. Special attention needs to be given to the established interest pattern existing among different levels of companies and employees. Moreover, establishing shared value, stringent corporate rules and regulations, training and other extracurricular activities are all important ways to facilitate the integration process (Ma et al., 2009).

However, the integration of values is by no means an easy job. As a long and enduring process, it requires enormous effort to improve internal communication, reshape the psychological contract among employees and enhance employee identity and trust (Li and Wei, 2008). As a matter of fact, communication has always been the key measure to ensure smooth implementation of the acquisition and the retention of key staff (Tang, 2007).

The organisation

Electronic Research Organisation (ERO) is a well-known company, manufacturing and selling video products, as well as undertaking research to continually improve the standard and quality of its products. The organisation has been operating for 55 years and has its head office in the US. Worldwide this company employs in excess of 8,000 people. In the Asia Pacific region, including China, the number of people employed is approximately 250. Those employees working in the Chinese operations are mainly sales and engineering support, as well as a small manufacturing division located in Shanghai.

They also have a research and development centre which supports three areas of the organisation; one part is carrying out research for US-based customers, the second supports the European market, and the third supports the Chinese market.

ERO was acquired by Network Systems, another United States based organisation. Network Systems is a network facilitation company, which tries to organise and coordinate various networks or departments within an organisation. The company is currently looking at more of an interactive environment where most functions can be done on one system, for example, a mobile phone, which will be a computer and can also operate home systems, such as video and audio hi-fi equipment. Previously many of these tools were only available for commercial purposes but both Network Systems and ERO are looking at providing these tools for home use. The term that the organisations are using for these facilities is 'home-connected services'. They both view this as a big potential area that many companies are tapping into. The employees of ERO think that their organisation was bought by Network Systems because of their specific expertise in video operation systems.

Most of the current customers of ERO are cable television operators. CNN is an example of one of their major customers. ERO provides the technology and the completed product, as well as the required software to this, and various other similar organisations. The success of the company has been assisted, not only by the high quality of the products, but also by the standard that the company provides in after-sales service to the customers.

Network Systems is a much younger company. The purchase of ERO created a number of issues that needed to be resolved. These included the impact of merging with another company on the corporate culture of the organisation, staffing numbers in the various departments, and the product mix. Because of the profitability of ERO, substantial interest in purchasing the organisation was expressed by many other companies. However, due to the assumed compatibility of the management style of Network Systems and ERO, Network Systems was the successful purchaser.

The problems

From a human resources perspective, Network Systems is viewed as a very strong organisation, being both profitable and fast-growing. However, its culture in some respects tends to be substantially different from ERO. For example, the average tenure of ERO employees is nine years, which is considered to be very high in this type of organisation. In contrast, the average tenure of Network Systems employees is only six years.

It is acknowledged that there is a fast turnover in Network Systems. For example, the Japanese, the Hong Kong, and the Korean HR managers have all resigned within the last two and a half years. The reason for their departure is not clear, but the implication coming through the informal communication channels (the grapevine) is the lack of support given to staff in Network Systems when dealing with employee problems. With ERO, however, there has been virtually no staff turnover. This indicates that ERO is possibly more conservative in its approach, but it is also a people-oriented organisation, providing support to staff working for them. People tend to work more closely, have better social connections, and tend to view the organisation as more of a family than do the employees of Network Systems. These tend to be the factors that drive people to stay with an organisation.

The leadership of ERO also tends to be more relaxed in its style. Leadership appears to be honest and also adopts a mentoring role with its staff. It also leads by example, by adopting a top-down approach. Substantial freedom and autonomy is given to staff in their research and provision of after-sales service, allowing them to make any necessary decision with the full support of management.

This is in direct contrast to Network Systems. While there is substantial people interaction at ERO, Network Systems uses minimal people interaction to resolve problems. It is more bureaucratic in its approach, tending to be more directive, not consulting with staff over problems that have occurred to determine the employees' views in resolving them. A critical issue, although this may be part of the strategy of the takeover bid, is that Network Systems has broken down many of the functions within the new organisation into smaller roles. In other words, it has reduced the scope of many jobs done by its staff through specialisation, which tends to reduce the skills usage of some employees. This affects the whole company, and although this 'scientific management' approach may work in a production company, in a research organisation it tends to be counter-productive across all sections of the business.

As an example, in the recruitment department of Network Systems, staff members concentrate solely on recruitment without taking on the broader aspects of advertising, selection and induction, as well as the performance management of those people. This means that people are doing a much narrower job than they could be doing within the organisation. Specialisation occurs as a result of this. They also hire many service providers to carry out a number of tasks for them. This tends to detract from the broader skills of many employees working within the HR department, and as a result they become too focused on one function. Many of the employees, of course, would prefer to perform a larger range of functions. This compares with ERO in which the HR department is responsible for recruiting, training, compensation, and industrial relations functions, among other roles. In other words, they adopt a more generalist function within the organisation. This provides greater opportunities to the employees to learn and develop their skills across the complete range of disciplines. By being challenged and given a broader range of tasks, the employees tend to be more motivated, less bored and subsequently are more keen to learn additional duties. Of course, there are advantages to specialisation, but within a small department, it helps if all employees have at least some basic knowledge and ability in other tasks that are carried out within a section in case of staff turnover.

The Chinese employees are very hard-working, and are also very keen to acquire new information that will assist them in their roles within the company. This broadening and providing of opportunities to the employees provide a better career path to the staff within the HR department. Specialisation tends to work against that approach, with resulting dissatisfaction and increased turnover.

An interesting perspective is that the company needs to attract the right people, but these are not necessarily the best people. By the best people, it is meant that employees join the organisation with high expectations and higher demands. In all types of jobs there are both challenging tasks and routine tasks. It is not always possible to provide challenging tasks to all employees. Someone must do the routine jobs, and to be fair these should be shared amongst all staff, who tend to appreciate this variation in labour.

To retain the best people can be costly to an organisation and also take great energy on the part of the management. It is better to hire staff who share a philosophy and have similar beliefs in the culture of the company, and to welcome into the organisation those people who are prepared to work at all levels, whether the work be challenging or routine. It is believed that these people are the ones that will stay with a company, whereas the best people are always looking for other opportunities in other organisations if they find that the work does not benefit or challenge them. The demands of these employees can be a high maintenance cost to the company.

It is very important to attract the right people to an organisation and to give them the correct work to match their abilities. In their daily duties it is most important to coach and guide them. Micro-managing an employee may not necessarily be the correct thing to do in today's environment. Many employees working in this type of organisation are highly intelligent and keen to learn. Because of this, it is not necessary to micro-manage them as they tend to be more self-motivated and will take initiative in their jobs.

Other issues like integrity and honesty cannot necessarily be managed. What needs to be done is to introduce processes that will encourage honesty and integrity in an employee. This is done by affective and honest leadership, through setting an example to staff from the top down, and understanding that people make mistakes and can be trained through effective mentoring. Hiring staff with potential to develop is possibly more important than hiring staff on their qualifications alone. From a human resources perspective, when hiring an employee into an organisation, the HR manager should be more interested in how that person will fit into the company. As regards the skill set, it is more the hiring manager's role to ask questions on that matter. The HR representative is really there to ascertain the person's character, their traits and their behaviour. The value system of the person is extremely important when they are joining a company, and through astute questioning and observation, this can be determined in many cases.

When hiring a new graduate, the organisation considered that it was preferable not only to look at the academic achievements of the applicant, as when they join an organisation they will be on a learning and development path to bring them to a suitable level of industry knowledge, but to look also at other activities that were undertaken by them while they were a student. These activities might include social or sporting events, or membership of clubs and societies within the university, which can lead to an identification of the character of this person, whether they are prepared to take on new challenges or additional work and whether they are capable of working in a team. These are some of the qualities that are looked for in addition to academic skills. These are also qualities that can assist the employer to judge whether the person is likely to remain within the organisation.

When employers look at where an employee or applicant has worked they look at the employing organisation itself, and what the person had done in that organisation by way of achievements. The problem with employing a person who has worked at a large number of organisations over a brief period of time is that these employees have repeatedly not been retained within the organisation either by their own choice or that of the company. They have not learned the skills or tasks that they have been given, they have not attained the necessary knowledge to broaden their depth of understanding of the tasks that they are performing, and they often have unrealistic expectations for compensation and benefits, believing that varied work experience is positive and desirable. These are the type of people that it is preferable not to hire, as they tend to have a very short retention within the company; after one or two years they will be gone in search of a promotion or better position.

The use of organisations as stepping stones is becoming quite common due to the higher expectations of many staff. The shortage of employees with appropriate skills is also contributing to this high turnover rate, as many companies, in their search for talent, are prepared to offer a higher salary or position to these employees. It may be noted that similar problems are occurring in many organisations in the growing Indian economy as well.

Mergers and takeovers

Apart from the differences in approach between Network Systems and ERO, many employees of Network Systems are becoming very uncomfortable with the roles they have been given. Staff at ERO feel that Network Systems is a numbers driven company; every Friday, the salespeople have to report back on their performance and state how many orders have been brought in over the past week. This tends to place extreme pressure on these staff to perform continually at a high level. It is felt that this pressure, among other things, will filter through to ERO employees as a result of the merger/takeover.

Furthermore, when Network Systems staff visit the ERO facilities, their approach tends to be more abrasive towards the ERO employees due to the frugal and cost-cutting culture within Network Systems. This has made many of the ERO employees very uncomfortable and unhappy with the takeover. But no effective communication plan has been implemented in the takeover to try to alleviate these concerns. Employees do not know what is to happen next, and to maintain the motivation of these employees communication is a very important tool. The integration process between Network Systems and ERO commenced in 2007, but communication skills were absent in the relationship. In the takeover negotiations, the feeling was that the employees were not being respected for the knowledge and experience that they had acquired in ERO, but rather in many instances were being treated as new employees, or were even being offered the same employment but with a reduction in salary.

This treatment tended to originate more from the managerial level. The view of staff was that there was mismanagement and disrespect of existing employees, which drove people away from the organisation, forcing them to look elsewhere for positions in which their knowledge and experience was respected. With the marketability and skills of these staff, there would be no problem in gaining new positions, at least for the local (Chinese) employees, considering the staff shortages that existed in many similar industries. With the expatriate employees, however, it was another matter of concern.

In ERO, there were a number of employees on expatriate packages. These employees came from other countries around the Asian region. However, as part of the takeover process, Network Systems wished to introduce localised packages for these employees. A localised package effectively means providing the expatriate with salary and conditions identical to the Chinese employees. While potentially being equitable to all staff, many expatriates brought with them valuable knowledge, skills and abilities, which have served to enhance the local industry, resulting in an increase of skills and knowledge that benefited the local workers directly, and the Chinese economy indirectly. A localisation proposal would result in a major reduction in salary and benefits for many of those existing expatriates who had remained within the company.

To alleviate the cut in benefits, pressure was then exerted by existing ERO employees for Network Systems to provide a 'soft landing' for many of these people. For example, some of the benefits that may have been provided to these employees included a better house and other associated perks. These were all incentives to attract valuable expatriate staff members to come and work in China. However, if employees move to the localised plan, they may need to look for cheaper housing or different schooling for their children. So the pressure was on Network Systems to provide compensation to those employees who were on certain expatriate benefits and privileges. Network Systems finally agreed to some extent on a 'softly-softly' approach to these talented staff members. Many of them, however, did look for other positions.

The takeover company has tended not to acknowledge the uniqueness of many ERO employees. This uniqueness is a result of the multi-tasking and multi-skilled approach that ERO took towards its employees, which allowed the company to use staff in a number of traditional and non-traditional areas, as the culture was one that led employees to believe in the approach to development being adopted by the organisation.

Student recruitment issues

An example of the two organisations' differences in recruitment can be demonstrated by their approach to student recruitment at universities. ERO tended to focus on students who had completed a Master's qualification, and offered a small number of places to these select students. The majority of the students accepted these places and commenced in a trainee position at ERO. The approach that ERO had adopted in their student recruitment exercises was for the managers, engineers and salespeople all to attend the recruitment fair, in other words, taking a holistic approach to recruitment, in which potential employees met the people that they may work or interact with at a future time.

In comparison, Network Systems made offers to up to 200 students but they could only get about 20 per cent of these to start work with them. There was always a high attrition rate due to their approach of using recruiting companies to visit the universities, instead of their own management and technical staff meeting with the students.

Expatriate leadership

Many companies also tend to tempt expatriate managers to become leaders in the new country, but this leadership often fails because of the attitude of the new managers towards the local employees. Many of the managers coming over take the view that they will only be there for a short time and any errors or mistakes that they make they attempt to hide. Unfortunately, the replacement manager then has to respond to these mistakes and try to fix them.

Corruption among some expatriate managers is also rife. The view of expatriates should be that they are there to contribute to the developing country, not to see what they can get out of the developing country. They are representatives of their own country. They also have to contribute to the society of the developing country. This should increase the level of trust between the different countries. Expatriates have to be good corporate citizens and become 'part' of the country. The mismatch that existed between a number of the expatriates of both organisations caused concern.

Industrial relations issues

In the past, China has adopted a top-down approach to regulation of employment. China has realised now, however, that it is important to sustain a growth economy into the future. Part of this philosophy is the need to treat all employees fairly. There has been substantial discussion about China dumping its cheap products in Europe and the United States. The Chinese government, however, is getting smarter by learning from this experience; although they have been providing cheap products to the world, they have also been polluting their own country to the detriment of the population.

China has now come up with new labour laws to improve the working conditions of its employees. This will make the working conditions of the population and the products produced by the workers more acceptable to many countries. There will be a signed contract between the employer and the employees. Welfare of the employees is of increasing importance, and they must be paid a minimum wage. This is to reduce exploitation of Chinese workers, both by local employers and also by multinational enterprises. The government is also driving out many of the heavy-polluting and labour-intensive companies to other, less populated and less environmentally sensitive areas. With the introduction of the new labour laws in 2008, the labour organisations have been empowered, so if a company does not have a labour union representing the employees they must form an employee representation group for any consultations affecting the employee. Any new policy or any new procedures or practices introduced within the company must go through the employee representation group.

They are also providing more power to the employee representative groups or the labour unions that exist within companies. Leaders need to be more involved in the day-to-day running of the companies. Since the joint venture between ERO and Network Systems came into being, management is now required to consult more widely with the labour union that exists in ERO. A regular dialogue has taken place as a result of the merger, in which the changes taking place and the effect of these changes on the employees have been regularly discussed with the union. This has been taking place over the last two years, with regular meetings between the human resources department and union members within the organisation. As a result there has been no union disputation as a consequence of the change. During this regular dialogue, new issues are always being brought up, but as a result of close communication, they have always been resolved to the satisfaction of both parties.

The union movement has become more involved in motivating employees and encouraging a positive attitude among its members. They are involved in all counselling, grievance and discipline issues within the company. The union chairman is invited in to these discussions. Also, to improve the family approach of the organisation, a social activities club was formed.

It must be noted that labour relations matters are gaining increasing importance within China generally. Managers need to be well exposed and well trained in understanding the changes in industrial relations that are occurring in the country. This includes both local and expatriate managers. It is expected as well that there will be further changes in the future, which will impact on employment law within China, thus improving working conditions overall.

Conclusion

Because of the approach taken by Network Systems to the takeover, it was regrettable that many of the senior managers and other staff members found that working for the new organisation was impossible. Many have left the company because of the attitude and approach of Network Systems to the ERO culture. Regardless of whether the merged company is successful or not, the new owners tend not to view the employees as an asset but rather as a disposable resource. A decision has to be made as to whether Network Systems is acquiring another company as a money-making resource, so it can be bigger than its competitors or expand in the field, or whether it is acquiring the culture of a successful organisation in the takeover. The reality is that it needs to be both to grow. If it only wishes to acquire the business and not the associated cultures that are part of the business, the organisation's take-over will fail, if not in the short term, certainly in the longer time frame.

This chapter examined an apparent clash of cultures, in which many policies and procedures were changed, but without adequate consultation with those affected. To maintain motivation and morale, especially in an advanced industry, staff need to be treated as people, and not ignored. The Chinese government is gradually tightening its approach to industrial matters, and this will affect not only local companies, but may make it more difficult to ignore employees during any organisational changes.

Finally, the approach adopted by ERO in recruiting sends messages to many companies both in China and internationally, where knowledge, skills and abilities may not necessarily result in the best person for the job. Fit within the culture needs to be recognised, to ensure that a good system is maintained.

References

Huang Sujian and Linghu An (2005) 'Post-merger integration: the key factor to the success of corporate merger and acquisition', *Economic Management*, **15**: 6–13.

Li Hai and Wei Hongguo (2008) 'Strategies and implementation of human resource integration in corporate mergers – the case of YH acquisition', *Human Resource Development of China*, **10**: 58–61.

Liao Quanwen and Li Hongbo (2003) 'Analysis of the drives, obstacles and optional models of the culture integration in mergers', *Management Sciences in China*, **16** (1): 33–37.

Ma Zhiqiang, Deng Bo and Zhu Yongyue (2009) 'Managing human resource conflicts in the merged company', *Science and Technology Management Research*, **6**: 455–457.

Peng Jiamin (2008) 'The construction of human resource competence after corporate acquisitions – the case of China Southern Airline', *Human Resource Development of China*, **5**: 63–66.

Peng Zhen (2004) 'The contribution of human resource integration in corporate acquisitions', *Human Resource Development of China*, **4**: 26–29.

Sun Jiajia and Wu Zheng (2009) 'An exploration into the human resouces factors affecting corporate merger and acquisition', *Human Resource Development of China*, **2**: 18–21.

Tang Bing (2007) 'Human resource management in different stages in corporate merger and acquisition', *Human Resource Development of China*, **7**: 101–103.

Tang Huamao and Feng Yucheng (2007) 'Risk of M & A based on core competence', *Economic Management in China*, **29** (11): 17–21.

Wu Tianzu and Chen Lihua (2006) 'Obtaining core technique by multinational merger & acquisition – the mode of cultivating the core competence of China's enterprises', *Science and Management of Science and Technology*, **4**: 139–143.

Yan Shimei and Wang Zhongming (2007) 'Research on the level and the pattern of human resource integration during the M & A intrapreneurship', *Journal of Zhejiang University (Humanities and Social Sciences)*, **37** (1): 178–189.

The compensation system reform of the multi-purpose workgroup in a heat-treatment workshop
Xie Yuhua

Introduction

This chapter examines a number of performance and compensation initiatives that have been introduced into a previously state-owned enterprise, which is now substantially privately owned. Some reluctance is displayed on the part of certain employees to accept the changes that are being introduced by the new director of the company. However, the director realises that if the company is to compete and remain successful and viable, changes need to occur.

Aspects of performance-related pay and the need to consult are discussed in this chapter. Also, a reluctance by many organisations to change is noted, which could lead in time to some companies failing, to be replaced by new organisations.

The organisation

Company A is a joint venture formed in 1994 by a Chinese state-owned car parts manufacturer and an American company specialising in car and motorcycle accessories, with 18 workshops operating in China and its main headquarters located in Beijing. It manufactures fuel injection pumps and aluminium castings for diesel automobiles, and exports these components to other countries. It has total assets of 700 million RMB, with the American partner holding 60 per cent of the shares and the Chinese partner holding the remaining 40 per cent. The main factory covers an area in excess of 210,000 square metres and employs more than 1,400 staff, 40 per cent of whom are professional technicians. It has more than 1,400 machines, both imported and locally-made equipment used for mechanical processing, testing, calibrating, detecting and experimenting. Its leading product is fuel injection pumps, with an annual production capacity of 350,000 pumps selling to several major car manufacturing groups and diesel engine manufacturers in China. The company enjoys a 30 per cent market share and is ranked as the second largest manufacturer in the industry in China.

Company A has 17 functional departments, two offices and nine workshops. There is a general manager, a deputy general manager, as well as nine vice presidents in charge of marketing, production, technology, procurement, HR, general administration, quality control, sales and legal.

Generally speaking, salaries in Company A are relatively high as compared to other local companies. Although the company is carrying out continuous reforms to establish a market-driven managerial system, due to its beginnings as a state-owned enterprise, the payment system in this company is more or less equality-based, regardless of each employee's performance. To be concise, it distributes the total pay for all of the workers to each workshop based on their total working hours and unit price of each hour. The workshop will then redistribute this pay to various working groups based on the same calculation method. The payment distribution among workshops and sub-workgroups is under the supervision of the company and each individual workshop, respectively.

The problems

In order to improve the fairness and efficiency of the current pay management system, and to give more discretion to the workshop in its pay distribution, Company A decided to carry out reforms to its pay management system in 2007. The reform in the heat-treatment workshop is described to illustrate the company-level reforms.

The heat-treatment shop employs 36 staff working over three shifts. Due to the nature of the heat-treatment process, it has a relatively long production cycle time. Moreover, the work intensity during the loading and unloading requires a team of more than two staff to work together, which leads to an equal treatment in the distribution of payment to these employees. Taking the multi-purpose furnace group as an example, this workgroup is critical for the workshop as well as for the company, having 14 staff undertaking 70 per cent of the heat-treatment processes. In the past, the salary was just based on attendance at work. Each staff member could get a fixed monthly allowance of 60 yuan (about 3–4 per cent of their monthly salary). After that, the least working hours among all group members is used as the base pay, and the members of the group could get an additional 15 yuan for each extra shift as a bonus. The group leader receives an additional 2 yuan per team member as the group leader allowance. The rest of the payment making up the total salary would be equally distributed among all group members.

This distribution approach brings with it a number of problems, including demotivated staff, which results in low production efficiency within the plant, as there are no incentives for the better workers, and very few group leader candidates, as people do not want the position due to the workload and the low salary weighting. If there was sufficient recognition through the salary and other benefits for the group leaders, there might be more interest in the role.

The present group leader of the multi-purpose furnace group in the heat-treatment workshop has been the group leader for two years. There are fourteen members in this group, of whom eight are furnace operators, responsible for maintaining and operating the equipment. Three are transferred from the 'bluing' group (part of the heat-treatment procedure) to assist the furnace-filling team because of the declining workload in 'bluing' and the increasing pressure that is being placed on the multi-purpose furnace group. The members of the 'bluing' group are happy about the move because they enjoy a pay rise due to the additional responsibilities that they are given. Apart from them, there are another three staff assisting the furnace-filling team. They are older and are near retirement. They had been doing some simple physical work and were transferred because the work was relatively easier to handle. They are as hard-working as in their previous positions. One of them had been the group leader previously. He is very eloquent and enjoys a certain personal influence among all of the workers.

The furnace operators normally spend less than 20 per cent of their working time operating and taking care of the equipment. It is required that furnace operators make preparations for furnace-filling with other group members in their non-operating time. However, they always try to slack off whenever they can, to avoid any of the difficult work. This practice tends to incur the discontent of the older group members.

The group leader is responsible for assigning work to group members. However, if the group leader leaves the meeting room, even for a short while, the group members will always go smoking and chatting in the restroom. The group leader tries to balance the workload between members but it takes him at least half an hour to persuade the members to accept the assignment each time. The three workers transferred from the bluing group are the only ones who show any initiative, because now they receive higher pay and, therefore, value the current position that they have been transferred to.

The solution

Seeing the inefficiencies, the newly-appointed workshop director, Mr Wang, decided to make some changes to boost the employees' morale. He decided to begin the changes in the multi-purpose furnace group as this is the most important procedure in the whole workshop, and he had noticed the attitudes of a number of the employees working there, and the problems that the team leader was having in getting the employees to work better. A series of three changes was proposed.

First, the director defined the responsibilities of the department. Due to the nature of the heat-treatment process, the necessity for continuous operation, the long production cycle, the work intensity and the need for a team-based approach, it was very difficult to work out specific individual position descriptions. However, the furnace operators and the assisting position responsibilities, and how the staff should cooperate with each other needed to be defined clearly.

Second, it was considered necessary to improve the equity of the compensation system on the principle of responsibility-based pay. Increasing pay for the positions that involved complicated skills, more responsibilities and risks was important. Due to the weighty responsibilities of the furnace operators, they received 15 per cent more of the working hours payment of those assisting workers for the same work time. This was effectively a pay increase based on the additional responsibility that the furnace operators had.

Third, measures to motivate all group leaders needed to be introduced. Using punctuality of delivery of the finished product, as well as quantity, quality, cost and safety as performance indicators to measure their performance were all considered appropriate. All of the indicators were weighted based on the importance of the operation. If the group leaders met all of those indicators successfully, they could get 200 yuan as additional incentive. However, if any serious accidents or quality defects happen, the group leaders will be penalised. These penalties could include a wage freeze and an award denial, depending on the severity of the problem.

The implementation

Mr Wang was very aware that employees tend to be very sensitive to any reform in the compensation system that imposes an immediate impact on an employee's personal interest. He knows that he has to be very careful in bringing in the changes and considerate of the necessity to consult with the staff.

Mr Wang decided he should get the employees' thoughts on the current and new compensation system. A number of them were very dissatisfied with the intended reform, but others supported the reform fully. Those who were dissatisfied were those who were reluctant to contribute to the operation. Nevertheless, the director still went ahead with the changes, despite the views of some of the staff.

Expecting the enhancement of production after the reform had been implemented, Wang spent several days considering how to persuade employees into accepting the new performance payment system to carry out the reform. From an opposition perspective, the three assisting furnace workers had succeeded in convincing the three bluing workers of the inequity of the payment system reform for all those working in an assisting role. Under pressure from the older staff, all the assisting workers in the workshop now opposed the reforms. This resulted in the progress of production being seriously impeded.

Soon after the problem arose, Mr Qin, the director's immediate superior, came to his office and confronted him: 'I heard from the employees that the salary distribution in your workshop went against the company rules. The group leaders receive several hundred allowances per month, while the team members receive less than 1,000 for the total package.'

Mr Wang explained to Mr Qin the details and reasons for his intended reform. Qin advised him to be especially cautious not to cause any over-reaction among the workers.

A few days later, the general manager held a meeting of the middle- to upper-level managers, advising them to tell all the departmental managers to be very careful in their salary distribution scheme, and to avoid arousing overreaction among employees, causing potential loss of production and reputation of the firm.

Mr Wang's reform proposal encountered difficulties and he was considering the implications of his attempt to make the salary and performance system more equitable and as a result, improve the culture and work ethic of his staff.

Conclusion

Despite the acceptance of many of the economic and work changes in China, as it becomes a rival to many of the developed economies, there is still a reluctance to introduce certain measures in some former state-owned enterprises that will enhance the production and efficiency of the company. The problem is how to introduce these measures while retaining the loyalty of employees, especially in areas in which there may be a skills shortage.

The problem is not assisted by senior management, who are comfortable with the old scheme and are themselves resisting change. Consultation is needed, but workers also need to realise that to retain their jobs, acceptance of different conditions may be needed. In many instances, although it is preferable to encourage acceptance of the change, in certain circumstances it may be necessary to impose change from the top down, with appropriate consultation with staff.

The balanced scorecard in the Credit Card Association of China

Introduction

The balanced scorecard was a development by Kaplan and Norton (1996), which led to a change in performance measurement in many organisations. Although there have been a number of improvements and changes to the approaches used, it has still been adopted by many companies worldwide, as a suitable performance management tool. The scorecard does this by translating a strategic framework into operational terms, examining financial, customer and internal business processes, learning and growth aspects, then highlighting objectives, measures, targets and initiatives to achieve goals.

Using the balanced scorecard as a model, the organisation discussed in this chapter, a major banking company in China, has been refocused and restructured to improve efficiency, accountability, customer service and employee morale. Duplication of duties was reduced and major training programmes were implemented, to better align the staff with the company's goals and objectives, through reconfiguring and affiliating the numerous departments via improved management and communication channels.

Literature review

Being an important tool of strategic and performance management, the balanced scorecard (BSC) plays a large role in organisations in finding balances between financial and non-financial indicators, long- and short-term goals, internal and external stakeholders, and leading and lagging indicators. It is also an efficient form of communication between managers and staff (An and Ge, 2004).

Xie and Yang (2008) studied a company's failed attempt in introducing the BSC and concluded that the reasons for failure were neglecting the inner connections among the four dimensions of the BSC, failure to be directed by corporate strategy, unquantifiable indicators in the BSC, and lack of supporting systems. Moreover, Song and Hu (2007) analysed reasons why the BSC failed in many organisations in China and concluded that lack of real support from top management, vaguely defined vision or strategy, carelessly designed job description, insufficient execution and obstructive corporate culture were all hindering factors in implementation of the BSC in Chinese enterprises.

In contrast, Ke and Ke (2005) explored the success factors in the implementation of the BSC in China Mobile and found that a clearly defined strategic goal, commitment from senior management in delegation and other supporting systems, top-down involvement (full participation), sufficient internal communication and regular revision and improvement of the BSC itself were the key factors contributing to the success. Similar suggestions were proposed by An and Ge (2004). Chen (2008) posited that a close link to corporate strategy, as well as more emphasis and weight on financial indicators or indicators contributing to financial performance, are essential to the success of the application of the BSC in profit-making companies.

In order to apply the BSC into strategic management, organisations may need to follow steps such as establishing a strategy map, designing measures, targets, and programmes of the BSC, implementing, collecting feedback, adjusting and revising the BSC system (Zhang and Cheng, 2004). Gao et al. (2006) discussed the application of the analytic hierarchy process (AHP) to deciding the weight among indicators in the BSC. Similarly, Zhu (2007) proposed a model of Enterprise Resource Planning (ERP) with the BSC, which applied AHP to the BSC to decide the weight distribution among BSC indicators, to measure the performance of ERP implementation.

Gao and Liu (2007) established a model of business technological innovation based on the BSC. Through the model, technological innovation could be planned, controlled, and managed by the BSC. In addition, risks from innovation can be effectively reduced, and innovation is made more efficient when directly connected with corporate strategies and performance.

Apart from this, several researchers studied the implementation of the BSC in different fields. Wu and Guo (2004) introduced the BSC into the government sector and established a framework for the application of the BSC in a public field. Huang and Lin (2006) discussed the application of the balanced scorecard in commercial banks through examining the performance evaluation systems of five commercial banks in China, and designed a new performance evaluation system for the banks based on the BSC. Shang et al. (2005) applied the BSC to an evaluation of the performance of research and development functions and developed a BSC performance evaluation system for research and development functions, whose performance assessment may be complicated due to its inherent uncertainty.

The organisation

The Credit Card Association of China (CCAC) is a national bankcard association, established a number of years ago with the approval of the government and a number of affiliated banking institutions. Its headquarters are located in Shanghai. Its role is to operate the unified bankcard transaction settlement system across a number of affiliated partners, thus providing participants in the bankcard sector with basic bankcard services, which include inter-bank information switching, settlement data processing, standards and regulations, and risk prevention strategies, among others. Its goal is to provide customers with high quality, safe and efficient bankcard services, and to maintain the security of the Chinese national financial information system through regular reporting to the government and the banking sector.

Since its establishment, CCAC has been consistently fulfilling industrial and social responsibilities to meet the increased card usage demand of the Chinese people. With CCAC's endeavours, China has become one of the countries with the fastest growth and the greatest potential for expansion in the bankcard industry. As of the end of 2007, over 150 CCAC domestic member banks issued more than 1.5 billion bankcards, among which 0.54 billion were CCAC standard cards. The number of domestic CCAC merchants totalled 740,000 with 1,180,000 POS terminals, and the number of ATMs reached 120,000, increases of 3.9, 4 and 2.5 times, respectively, since the end of 2001 (prior to CCAC's establishment).

Bankcards are widely accepted by merchants in medium and large cities, and the number of merchants accepting bankcards in small cities is also increasing rapidly. Furthermore, CCAC cards are now accepted in 26 countries and regions frequently visited by Chinese people on business or holidays. Currently, over 14 million inter-bank transactions are processed daily with a transaction volume in excess of 10 billion RMB. CCAC has made significant achievements in inter-operability, brand building and internationalisation, and effectively promoted rapid and sound development of the Chinese bankcard industry.

CCAC has so far begun offering its card services in 24 countries and regions, namely, Hong Kong, Macau, Singapore, Malaysia, Thailand, Japan, Korea, Germany, France, Spain, Belgium, Luxembourg, The Netherlands, Italy, Switzerland, Turkey, United States, Australia, New Zealand, Kazakhstan, Indonesia, Philippines, Vietnam and Russia. This makes it possible for CCAC cards to be used on the ATM network of Citibank in 36 countries and regions throughout the world. In Hong Kong, more than 90 per cent of ATMs are now compatible with CCAC cards.

Company mission and responsibilities

As China's bankcard association, CCAC has become a crucial and pivotal part of the bankcard industry, and plays an essential role in the realisation of interconnection between bankcard systems. Relying on the Credit Card Association's inter-bank transaction settlement system, the association promulgates and promotes the access standards of the CCAC inter-bank transaction settlement system to unify bankcard inter-bank technology standards and service specifications, and to form a resource-sharing and self-disciplining mechanism for the bankcard industry, so as to conduct, coordinate, advance and promote the development of the industry. Commercial banks realise interconnection and resource-sharing between systems through the transaction settlement system of the Credit Card Association of China to ensure the inter-bank, inter-region and cross-border usage of bankcards is conducted safely.

The main responsibilities of CCAC include establishing and operating the BankPay inter-bank transaction settlement system, and promoting the unified bankcard standards and specifications. CCAC also provides basic bankcard services, such as inter-bank information exchange, settlement data processing and risk prevention to commercial banks, merchants and cardholders, and promotes the intensive and scale development of the bankcard industry. Together with the commercial banks, CCAC has assisted in establishing a number of proprietary bankcard brands.

The problems

Since its establishment, CCAC has experienced rapid expansion, with the number of departments growing from three to currently more than twenty. At the very beginning of the CCAC startup, departments were set up based on different projects. A new department would be established when certain activities or projects needed to be done. The structure of the company was not a very efficient one and there existed a certain overlap of responsibilities among departments within the organisation. As a result of this duplication of duties in a number of departments, CCAC decided to restructure itself to reduce this inefficiency.

CCAC is basically a hierarchical structure, with the president's office working below the board of directors and the board of supervisors. All the departments and regional branches report to the president's office directly (see Appendix 1). This structure should ensure efficiency as well as smooth vertical communication and has contributed substantially to the success of CCAC in its early development.

However, as CCAC expanded rapidly, strong collaboration between departments became indispensable to guarantee the fulfillment of bigger projects. Initially, the departments were more than capable of accomplishing their own tasks and rarely exchanged information or communicated with other departments. They reported the implementation of their plans and any difficulties that they encountered to the president directly, which caused low efficiency in horizontal communication and tardiness in problem-solving. Performance appraisal was satisfactory at a departmental level, but poor at the company level. The departments may have achieved their goals respectively, but collectively failed to hit the corporate goal.

How to ensure the implementation of corporate strategies and boost inter-departmental cooperation was a real challenge facing the company. Incorporation of horizontal communication and accomplishment of corporate goals into the performance evaluation system was considered a good way out. However, being a subjective criterion, communication and coordination are very difficult to measure quantitatively. The challenge was how to link corporate goals with departmental goals and integrate the contribution of those departments toward the realisation of corporate strategies.

To boost the inter-departmental communication – the horizontal committee system

In order to promote and strengthen horizontal communication and coordination among departments, CCAC established nine horizontal committees, with six of them handling internal operations, namely the remuneration and assessment committee, the auditing committee, the operational management committee, the dispute resolution committee, the risk management committee and the market development committee. The other three were the technical experts committee, the information security committee and the bankcard service advisory committee, playing a consulting role and providing suggestions to the President's Office on important decisions affecting the organisation (see Appendix 1).

The six committees operate independently from all the departments and branches and report directly to the board of directors. All the committee members are part-time and are members of different departments. The director of the committee is generally a member of a certain department, but not a department head. He/she has the right to request one part-time member from each department to work in conjunction with him/her. All the committee members joined the committee voluntarily. They are responsible for communicating and coordinating in the related fields among departments. They are fully delegated from the board and have the authority to demand cooperation from any department head. The president requires all the departments to cooperate and support the committees and assesses the committees' performance by the final outcome of their job without any interference in their daily work.

CCAC provides training on a variety of topics, including project management and communication skills, to all the committee members. The board requires all the departments' heads to provide support and necessary resources to the committee members in their work plan and schedule. The training centre needs to inform the departments of the training programmes and schedule in advance. To ensure the smooth cooperation of the departments, the general manager requests that the training centre provides a written report on the implementation of the training programmes, and the support and cooperation given by the departments after each programme has been completed. An online learning website is available to all the committee members with different access rights. All the training courses have a start date and are available during certain periods. Below is a sample of some of the training courses that are available online.

- Advanced data management in Excel 2002
- MS Outlook 2000 preliminary course
- Office etiquette
- Defect management
- Preparing efficient business meetings

- Telephone skills
- Efficient e-mail communication
- Performance evaluation
- Develop potentials for autonomous learning
- Fitting in the team
- Time management
- Improving communication skills and maintaining team morale
- Problem-solving and decision-making in the team
- Preparing for the new managerial role
- Problem-solving and conflict resolution
- Leadership
- Stress management
- Promoting standard CCAC card
- International CCAC card – operation procedure and specifications for merchants.

The performance of the committee members is reviewed by both their department head and the director of the committee. Their pay is directly linked with their workload and the results of the performance review.

To align corporate goals with departmental activities – the balanced scorecard

To monitor its overall performance as an organisation, CCAC decided to adopt the balanced scorecard approach in 2005. By looking at larger-scale corporate objectives, BSC helps CCAC to measure performance from multiple perspectives and to integrate all departments toward the corporate goal. CCAC established the BSC from four classic perspectives: financial, customer, internal process, learning and growth (see Table 8.1).

The answers to each key question become the *objectives* associated with that perspective. Before any objectives are decided, a thorough analysis of the strengths, weaknesses, opportunities and threats (SWOT) is conducted to diagnose the internal and external environment of CCAC (see Figure 8.1).

Table 8.1	Perspectives and questions

Perspective	Key question
Financial	To succeed financially, how should we appear to our stakeholders?
Customer	To achieve our vision, how should we appear to our customers?
Process	To satisfy our customers and shareholders, at what business processes must we excel?
Learning and growth	To achieve our vision, how will we sustain our ability to change and improve?

Figure 8.1   The development process of the BSC in the CCAC

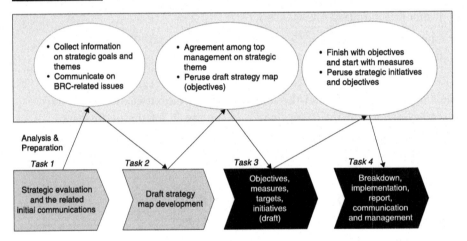

SWOT analysis of the CCAC

Strengths:

- support from the government (before the full opening of the domestic market);
- integration of state-of-the-art technology in the world;
- inter-bank networks and institutions covering the whole of China;
- relative low costs and comprehensive advantage in service procedure integration;
- local advantages in the possibilities of obtaining additional resources;

- organisational learning capacity and a strong will for innovation.

Weaknesses:

- underdeveloped market, limited use of bank card for payment, credit card is just taking off;
- no international brand;
- global network needs to be perfected;
- insufficient funds to further develop the local market;
- management standards and operational practices are not up to international level;
- connection with banks needs to be further enhanced;
- small number of cards issued in the market, insufficient market share, lagged product standards and development.

Opportunities:

- China is the bankcard market with the most growth potential in the world;
- e-payment system is a sunrise industry with wide prospects and scale effect;
- global bank card market is currently restructuring, the dominance of Visa and Master Card is facing challenges.

Threats:

- transition businesses will face a severe challenge if global competitors establish their own transition network in China after the full de-regulation of the domestic market;
- threat of losing market share to competitors (Visa, Master) if the CCAC brand has not been fully established before the deregulation of the domestic market.

The establishment of a strategy map

After deciding on four strategic perspectives and scanning the internal and external environment, it became important to link the perspectives, objectives and measures. To help to communicate large, complex quantities of information in simple, easily understood ways, a strategy map was adopted by the company (Figure 8.2).

Figure 8.2 The strategy map

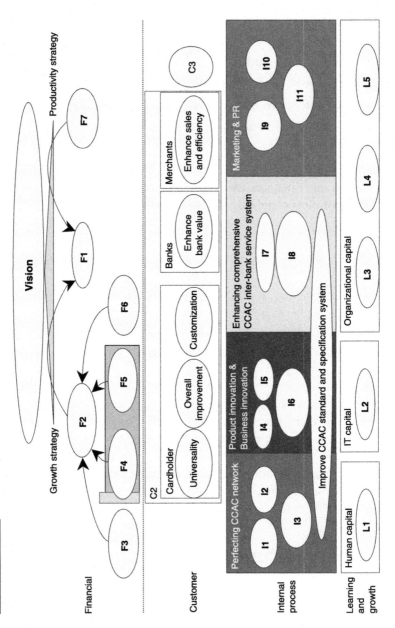

This helped to align each level of the organisation with the overall strategy by providing a visual way to communicate to different parts of the organisation and showing how they all fit into the overall strategy. It assisted in cascading the BSC through the organisation, since it can be generated at different organisational levels.

Breakdown of the strategy map – strategic objectives

The strategy map was broken down into a number of strategic objectives, with appropriate goals described. Broadly the objectives focused on the four areas of financial, customer, internal process and learning and development (see Table 8.2).

The creation of a strategy matrix

The strategy matrix displays objectives, measures, targets and initiatives in one table (Table 8.3). The progress towards achieving an objective is

Table 8.2 Strategic objectives

From a financial perspective	
Strategic objective	Descriptions
F1. Return for shareholders	Focus on both short-term and long-term benefits for shareholders. Better fulfilment of social responsibilities in the process of continuous growth of corporate value. These will help CCAC acquire support. CCAC will bring shareholders long-term benefits through increasing inter-bank transition income and slashing cost.
F2. Raise income from inter-bank transition network	Operating the standardised national inter-bank information exchange network will become CCAC's core business and financial foundation to realise its strategic goals. In the short run it could be realised through increasing the public use of the bank card and collecting reasonable fees, in the long run through issuing more standard CCAC cards and boosting the trading volume of those cards.

Continued

Table 8.2	Strategic objectives (*contd.*)
F3. Promote usage of bankcard among the public	Enhance the ratio of bankcard trading in the total retail sector, promote the replacement of bankcard for cash trading. This is CCAC's social responsibility and will help CCAC expand its market share. CCAC will continually increase the use and expand the usage of the bankcard through improving the function and coverage of its network, enhancing the universality and value-added service of the bankcard, and boosting the public awareness of it as well as winning government support.
F4. Increase the issuance of standard CCAC card rapidly	CCAC needs to seize more market share and reach more high-end customers through offering customised products/services. Promoting standard CCAC cards plays a vital role in consolidating the dominance of CCAC in the inter-bank transition industry and thus will be the core of its medium-term strategy. CCAC will accomplish this goal by putting more emphasis on the market, developing well-received standard cards products and improving the standard CCAC card service system.
F5. Boost trading volume of the standard CCAC card	Constantly increase the proportion of standard CCAC cards in the total bankcard trading, which is a key criterion deciding the dominance of standard CCAC cards. CCAC will endeavour to make it first choice for the card holders by offering tailored value-added service and enhancing trading volume of its standard card.
F6. Reasonable charging system	Grow business through establishing a reasonable fee charge system and pricing standard.
F7. Integrate services to cut down cost	CCAC will take advantage of its network to achieve cost advantages in its transition business by integrating service efficiently in a cost saving way. This is a strategic direction for CCAC to expand cost-efficiently.
From customer perspective	
Strategic Objective	**Description**
C1. Increase market presence of the standard CCAC card and CCAC network	See F2, F4 and F5

Table 8.2 Strategic objectives (*contd.*)

C2. Customer satisfaction	Card universality	Card universality is the foundation of inter-bank business. It is important to ensure that the standard CCAC card can be used at any time, any place and in any way. CCAC will improve this through expanding its network in different regions, industries and payment channels.
	Overall Improvement	Continually improve service quality in the inter-bank exchange and settlement processes to ensure successful trading. This is closely related to CCAC's brand image and will be realised through improvement in technology, management, organisation and regulations.
	Customised service	Provide cardholders with a variety of products and value-added service, assisting the standard CCAC card in out-competing international brands in local functions. CCAC will achieve this through making alliances with other product and service suppliers and meanwhile strengthen integrated service for banks and merchants.
	Enhance bank value	Provide to banks products that may increase card trading, make a strategic alliance and hold joint promotion on card products with banks, and offer specialised service for banks. Enhancing bank value is a prerequisite to popularising the standard CCAC card. CCAC will introduce a series of standard CCAC products and services to meet the needs of banks and cardholders to the maximum extent.
	Enhance sales and efficiency	Help merchants boost income through more sales, cut down cost related to cash trading for them, as well as enhancing payment efficiency. Merchant benefits are the basis of network construction. CCAC will strive to create value for merchants through improving network efficiency, promoting a standard CCAC card and expanding card consumption.
C3. Establish a reliable E-payment brand		It is the core of CCAC's mid-term strategy that it becomes the payment brand of choice for domestic cardholders and gradually becomes a well-known international e-payment brand among foreign cardholders. To achieve this, CCAC will continue expanding its network and promoting CCAC products and relevant service.

Continued

Table 8.2	Strategic objectives (*contd.*)

From an internal process perspective

Perfecting CCAC network

Strategic Objective	Description
I1. Exploration of domestic market	Exploring the market by expanding payment channels and into more regions and application fields to form the network foundation of CCAC brand.
I2. Enhance network efficiency	Enhance inter-bank trading efficiency and quality and ensure network safety, efficiency and continuous operation. CCAC will emphasise network construction by strengthening inspection, detection, information circulation and by improving quality measures by reducing defects, disputes, complaints, and through improved risk management.
I3. Develop an international channel for standard CCAC card	Expanding standard CCAC card network internationally. CCAC will make a vigorous effort to form a strategic alliance with acquirers abroad to develop an international acceptance channel for the CCAC card.

Product innovation and business innovation

Strategic Objective	Description
I4. Develop new payment channel	Establishing multi-channel payment by promoting Internet payment, mobile payment, telephone payment and STB (set top box) payment will help CCAC promote its products and services. CCAC will do so through coordination with other companies in the relevant fields.
I5. Technological innovation in e-payment	In order to ensure leading technology in the e-payment field, CCAC should enhance its technological R&D capacity to provide strong backup for product and business innovation. Only through this can CCAC achieve sustainable development. CCAC will accomplish this goal through forming an R&D team, increasing R&D input and keeping abreast of the updates in the international e-payment field.

Table 8.2   Strategic objectives (*contd.*)

I6. Develop a series of standard CCAC card products	Developing products that cater to customer needs is the key to promoting the standard card. Based on the specific needs of the market segments and marketing strategy of issuing banks, CCAC will strive to satisfy cardholders' needs through R&D staff training, strengthening market research and continuously developing new products with different functions.
Enhancing comprehensive CCAC inter-bank service system	
Strategic Objective	**Description**
I7. Improve professionalised service system	Establish an acquiring system that meets the expectation of banks and merchants, provides for bank marketing, cardholder information services and relevant data processes, continually improve the issuing and marketing environment for card issuers. This is the foundation for CCAC to consolidate and further develop inter-bank transactions and will be realised through integrating social resources and enhancing the operational efficiency of subsidiaries.
I8. Improve service system for cardholders	Offer comprehensive basic and value-added services to cardholders. Depending on its subsidiaries, customer service centre and other issuing and acquiring institutions, CCAC will pay close attention to every service link including inter-bank transactions, dispute settlement, complaint handling, risk precaution and information service, so as to construct a comprehensive cardholder service system and to constantly improve transaction and service quality.
Improve CCAC standard and specification system	Establish a comprehensive standard and specification system in line with international practice with independent intellectual property rights, including business and technical specifications for card types, payment channels, payment policy, and payment tools. This is an indispensable element for CCAC to improve its network, achieve product and business innovation, and construct a comprehensive service system. CCAC will expedite the construction of this system and endeavour to promote the thorough implementation of it.

Continued

| Table 8.2 | Strategic objectives (*contd.*) |

Marketing and PR	
Strategic Objective	**Description**
I9. Increase marketing effort in promoting standard CCAC card and other new products and services	CCAC will focus on promoting its standard card and new products and services to issuing banks or help issuing bank to assist the cardholders, and in doing so, collect feedback on products from the market, providing improvements and innovation ideas for R&D department. This is where CCAC could practically realise the goal of promoting the standard card and will be realised through attracting more marketing professionals and increasing marketing input.
I10. Establishing rapport with governments, stakeholders and the general public	CCAC will make every effort to establish and maintain good public relations through good publicity, communication with the general public, trying to obtain agreement and policy support from government, stakeholders and the public.
I11. Boost CCAC brand awareness and reputation	Make CCAC a household brand through business activities, advertising and other public welfare activities, attracting more potential customers to adopt the standard CCAC card.
From a learning and growth perspective	
Strategic Objective	**Description**
L1. Cultivate and attract strategic talent	In order to meet requirements of current and future development, CCAC will focus on cultivating and attracting three kinds of professionals, including managerial talent, technical talent and international talent.
L2. MIS construction	CCAC will establish an integrated MIS to take better use of information, facilitate information flow, promote operational efficiency, and support decision-making. MIS is needed to realise the centralised management and sharing of information and to further promote information sharing in CCAC.
L3. Best practice in management	CCAC will improve managerial practice by restructuring and reengineering business procedures if necessary, and implement dynamic management of corporate strategies to ensure strategy execution.

Table 8.2   Strategic objectives (*contd.*)

L4. Customer oriented corporate culture	Customer-oriented culture guarantees the competitiveness of CCAC. CCAC will stay closely aligned with customers in product development, marketing and service providing, striving to offer high-quality products and services out of understanding and continuously exploring the needs of banks, merchants and cardholders.
L5. Coordination within the company	Emphasising cooperation among departments within the company to achieve synergy. Define the role of the relationships among departments and branches in the group corporation through resource allocation, keeping all the subsidiaries on track towards achieving the goal of CCAC, reducing costs and thus enhancing the total competitiveness of CCAC in market competition.

Table 8.3   The strategy matrix

	Objective	Measure	Initiative
Financial	■ Maximised return ■ Profit growth ■ Business lever ■ Control on operational cost	■ Return on assets ■ Revenue growth ■ Asset utilisation rate ■ Operational cost per customer	
Customer	■ Leading customer satisfaction in the industry	■ Customer satisfaction	■ Customer satisfaction project
	Core business optimisation		
	■ Core product optimisation ■ Maximised return from resource allocation ■ Continuous cost management ■ Company-wide risk management	■ % revenue brought by low-standardised product/service ■ Revenue through new service ■ % service provided through alliance or joint venture ■ NPV brought by product/service ■ % Draft decisions in R&D meetings	■ Telecommunication infrastructure construction ■ Trading risk evaluation ■ Research projects coordination ■ Proactive and protective measures

Continued

Table 8.3	The strategy matrix (*contd.*)

	Constant PR support		
Internal process	▪ Network management ▪ Reliable service ▪ Customer communication and training	▪ Customer/partner satisfaction (5-point scale) ▪ Reliability index ▪ Communication/ training coverage (%) ▪ % communication/ training programme implementation	▪ Community projects
	Customer service enhancement		
	▪ Smooth cross-BU service ▪ Understand customer motivation ▪ Efficient customer service	▪ % On-time delivery rate ▪ Proportion of new product usage ▪ Proportion of on-time market research ▪ Customer satisfaction – C.S. centre (see results above) ▪ Problem-solving time – customer service centre	▪ Two-way transaction market project ▪ Service automation ▪ Information system up-grading ▪ Call centre software integration ▪ Maintenance benchmarking ▪ Shared service benchmarking/ out-sourcing programme ▪ ERP implementation
	Business development		
	▪ Return bought by low-level utilisation ▪ Business opportunity optimisation ▪ Service innovation	▪ % proportion of projects reaching rated production capacity ▪ Increase rate of staff productivity ▪ % cost reduction ▪ Shut-down cost and plan ▪ System recovery time	

	▪ Introduce alliance programme and joint project ▪ Coordination between cross-BU R&D		
Learning and growth	▪ Ensure market driven ▪ Leading employee satisfaction ▪ World-class leadership	▪ Coverage rate of strategic competence ▪ Time-length of training on strategic competence ▪ Customer satisfaction (5-point scale) ▪ Effectiveness of leadership (5-point scale)	▪ Competitiveness description ▪ Performance-related pay ▪ Leadership training programme

Table 8.3 The strategy matrix (*contd.*)

evaluated by measures (see Figure 8.3). An objective is likely to be gauged by more than one measure and normally different weights are assigned to multiple contributing measures. An initiative is an action plan designed to achieve objectives. The initiative helps to move a measure toward its target value.

Five criteria to evaluate the effectiveness of the measures

The following five criteria were measured using a five-point scale from very effective (1) to not effective at all (5).

Strategic communication:

▪ Can this measure help strategic decision-makers understand how well strategies are being carried out and communicate the outcomes to employees? Will it lead to the expected behaviours among employees? Does it focus on the realisation of the strategies or generate other negative effects, such as diverting employee attention to other issues or causing a negative effect on corporate performance?

Figure 8.3 The screening of measures and initiatives

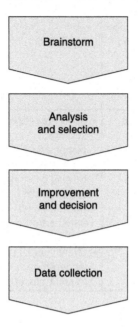

Effectiveness:

- Is it quantifiable? Are there measurable goals to assess the improvement of performance (clear performance expectation)?

Repetitiveness:

- Can the data from it be collected repetitively? If yes, is it better to collect monthly or quarterly?

Data collection:

- Does the measure still make sense in the industry as time goes by? Is the data collected objective and reliable? What is the cost of the data collection process?

Responsibility:

- Can it clearly define responsibilities by 'cascading down' the measures? Can the responsibilities be specified under this system?

Six criteria for screening initiatives

Again these six criteria were assessed on a five-point scale ranked from very high (1) to very low (5).

Consistency:

- support to the strategic goal;
- impact on the measure and goal.

Effectiveness:

- strength of organisational competence and competitive advantages formed;
- length of time to produce desired results.

Investment:

- amount of input needed.

Resources:

- resources needed during implementation;
- difficulty in acquiring the necessary resources.

Difficulty:

- difficulty in implementation;
- length of time needed for implementation.

Risk:

- changes entailed by the plan and their negative impact on company operations;
- length of time needed for implementation;
- difficulty in acquiring key technology and methodology.

Sample matching grid of initiatives

The matching grid can point to areas where scorecard elements might be out of balance. For example, there may be a cluster of initiatives around one objective, while other objectives have no supporting initiatives (see Fig. 8.4).

Table 8.4 Template for an initiative

Name of initiative:	
Sponsor:	Person liable: who manages the action plan
Starting date: of action plan	Deadline: duration and finishing date
Description: detailed description of the project	
Impact on strategy: list the strategies influenced by the project	
Impact on profit: describe how the project influences corporate profit (finance/customers)	
Remarks and assumptions	
Impact on competence: describe how the project influences procedure and corporate practice	
Risks: describe major risks involved in fulfilling the plan	
Critical support: list other plans or activities necessary to fulfil this action plan	Resources: list the required budget, man-hour, person, equipment, etc.
Milestones	Descriptions
1st quarter	
2nd quarter	
3rd quarter	
4th quarter	

Conclusion

As the company expanded, it realised that it needed an effective performance measure to ensure that its goals and objectives were met. The implementation of a balanced scorecard to measure performance from a number of perspectives worked well in focusing the company towards meeting specific targets, and also giving it information to expand further in the financial and banking sector. The action plan resulting from the BSC also provided the company with a positive direction.

The expansion of the industry in the Chinese market has been assisted greatly by the performance measures adopted, and the rationalisation of the management structure has shaped the company for many of the changes that will occur.

Figure 8.4 Matching grid

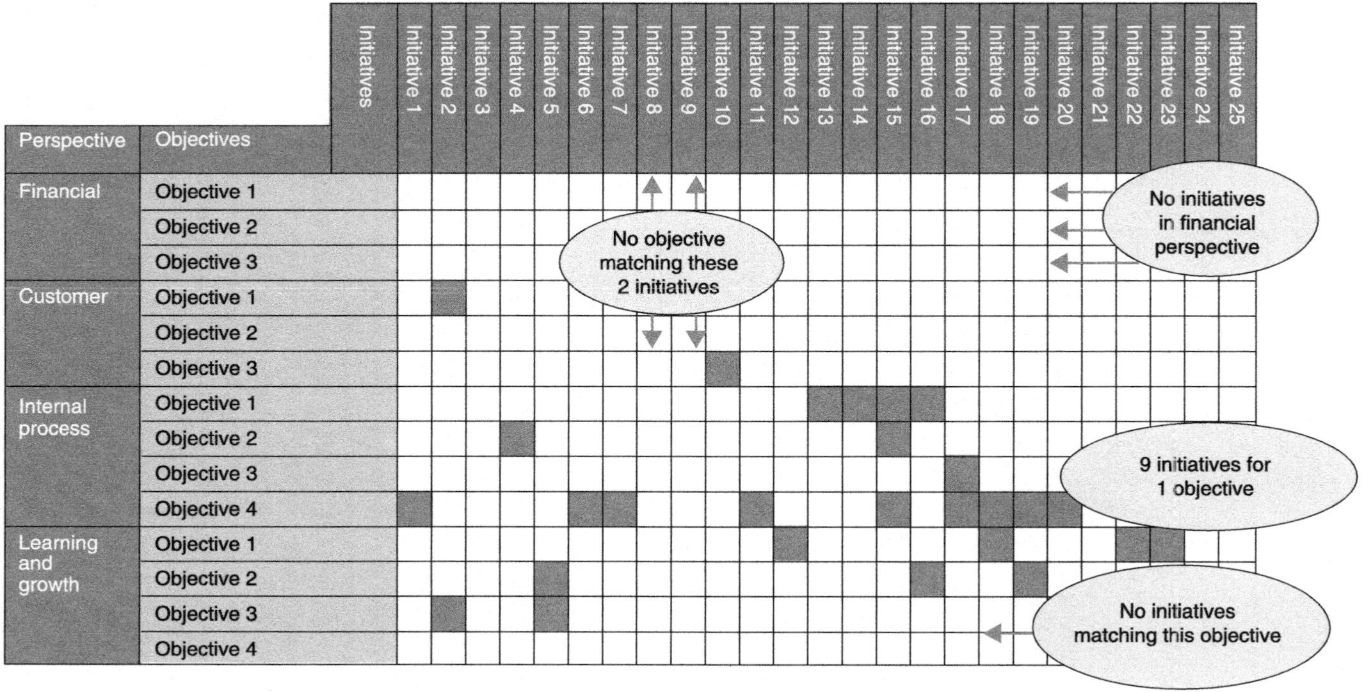

Appendix: The organisational structure of CCAC

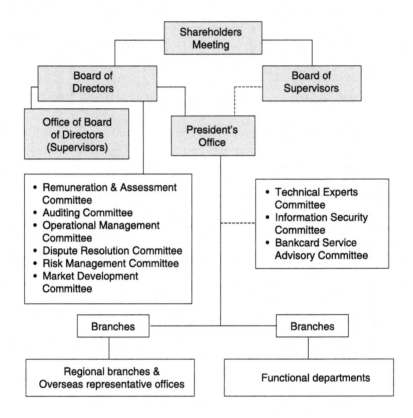

References

An Hongzhang and Ge Junfeng (2004) 'An all-around analysis of BSC', *Human Resource Development of China*, 9: 48–52.

Chen Liang (2008) 'Company's strategy, value adding and BSC', *Economic Management*, 30(18): 50–53.

Gao Deshan, Zheng Shaofeng and Liao Zhenghua (2006) 'The determination of the weight among indicators in the performance measurement system of balanced scorecard', *Contemporary Economy and Management*, 28(3): 125–128.

Gao Xirong and Liu Wei (2007) 'A model of technological innovation based on balanced scorecard', *Science Research Management*, 28(2): 66–70.

Huang Huixin and Lin Xiaochi (2006) 'From strategy to action: the balanced scorecard for commercial banks', *Journal of Beijing Institute of Technology (Social Sciences Edition)*, 8(3): 62–65.

Kaplan, R. and Norton, D. (1996) *The Balanced Scorecard*. Harvard Business School Press, Boston, USA.

Ke Lijia and Ke Lifei (2005) 'Critical success factors in the implementation of balanced score card in China Mobile', *Enterprise Management*, **11**: 37–39.

Shang Rubin, Tang Zhenhui and Wen Guibing (2005) 'Utilizing the balanced scorecard for R&D performance evaluation', *Science of Science and Management of S&T*, **4**: 15–18.

Song Wenwu and Hu Guoliang (2007) 'Performance management under balanced scorecard', *Modern Management Science*, **3**: 100–101.

Wu Jiannan and Guo Wenjing (2004) 'The causal analysis of realizing performance targets: an application of balanced scorecard in local governments', *Management Review*, **16**(6): 22–27.

Xie Lingling and Yang Wenchao (2008) 'A case in failed application of BSC and its solutions', *Human Resource Development of China*, **6**: 51–66.

Zhang Zigang and Cheng Zhiyong (2004) 'Application of balanced score card to strategic management', *Chinese Journal of Management*, **1**(3): 277–280.

Zhu Xuezhen (2007) 'Assessing strategic performance of ERP implementation', *Economic Management in China*, **29**(9): 50–54.

Staff turnover in a pharmaceutical and healthcare company

Introduction

The organisation is a multinational pharmaceutical and healthcare supply company, with its main Chinese operation located in Shanghai. With a change of management and a reordering of priorities, this has led to substantial dissatisfaction among sales staff, who fear that their autonomy is threatened due to an increasing emphasis on management systems. This change of management style by the new general manager has resulted in a high staff turnover among sales staff due to, among other things, loss of income as a result of increased competition among other healthcare supply companies and the new managerial approach being introduced.

Resulting from these changes, a major recruiting campaign needed to be undertaken. Additionally, a number of other initiatives were introduced, including an emphasis on educating staff in the core values of the company, motivational initiatives, increased communication and accountability, and a performance system that placed greater pressure on the sales staff. New staff members who were joining the company were also provided with a more effective introduction in their orientation programme.

Literature review

Turnover factors are generally characterised as personal, company-related, family-related, or external environmental reasons (Hu et al., 2007; Xu, 2007; Zhang and Yang, 2009). However, reasons for turnover may vary depending on the nature of the organisation. A survey conducted in an electrical enterprise identified 10 factors influencing turnover in Chinese stated-owned organisations undergoing major changes. These factors were age, political party affiliation, educational background, tenure, professional titles, working departments, position characters, administrative ranks, rewarded times and training received (Zhang and Jing, 2006). For the fast-responding knowledge-based enterprises, high educational level, younger age, fewer promotion opportunities due to the flat structure, too much focus on technology, less commitment due to a lack of personal communication, and deficient performance management systems may be the most significant reasons leading to staff turnover (Hu et al., 2007). Zhang (2008) surveyed 25 hi-tech enterprises in Xi'an (in the northwest part of China) and found that career development was the crucial factor influencing key staff turnover, followed by management expertise, work relations and personal qualifications, with the level of remuneration and the working environment exerting a weak influence on the turnover. Contrary to these views, Wang et al. (2008) found in an empirical study among hi-tech enterprises that the remuneration factor was the most weighted factor influencing staff turnover, with career development and employee commitment in second and third place. Other researchers identified more contributing factors such as an increased preference for external recruiting by the company rather than promotion from within, a greater emphasis placed on vertical advancement while ignoring position rotation to enhance comprehensive experience of the staff, and lack of internal equity in incentive systems (Zhao, 2009).

Accordingly, researchers proposed various suggestions to reduce unnecessary turnover rate. Career development plans may be the most frequently mentioned approach to retain staff (Hu et al. 2007; Zhang, 2009), with multiple career paths suggested to help employees achieve their individual career goals without leaving the organisation (Zhao, 2009). The management of the psychological contract has also been proposed by several researchers (Zhao and Zhao, 2004; Wang et al., 2008). To successfully achieve this, establishing the psychological contract from the recruiting process, providing real-time guidance for employees to modify and consolidate it, promoting equity to emphasise it, and establishing smooth communication channels have been suggested (Liu and Wang, 2009; Bian, 2005). In addition, Xu (2007) proposed delegation and self-managed teams, and the establishment of a learning culture within the organisation as important ways to motivate and therefore retain knowledgeable workers.

Although there has always been debate about the extent to which financial incentives can motivate employees, no one is denying the motivating role of suitable compensation packages. Both Zhang (2009) and Ma (2004) mentioned the significant and cost-efficient role of the flexible use of remuneration packages in motivating and keeping staff. To do this, establishing a cafeteria total rewards system could be useful (Zhao, 2009). Another important factor is the balance of internal equity and external competitiveness, which seems to be crucial in designing payment systems (Ma, 2004; Zhang, 2009).

Other suggestions include establishing acting positions before formal promotion (Zhao, 2009), promotion of participative management style and an emphasis on intrinsic motivation with non-institutionalised incentives (Zhao and Zhao, 2004). Companies need to recruit people who can fit into the organisation at the very beginning (Zhang, 2009) and then treat their employees as their 'internal customers' (Hu et al., 2007).

The organisation

The organisation is a multinational company operating in more than 50 countries, with in excess of 250 subsidiaries. It is on the cutting edge in its development of new healthcare products and takes a highly ethical approach to its products and treatment of its customers. It considers that its reputation is its greatest asset and it takes pride in its delivery of products and its caring approach to staff, customers and the environment.

China and Subsidiaries Medical Supplies (CSMS) is the Chinese branch, with its head office located in the United States and its Chinese office in Shanghai. There are also representative organisations in other cities in China. These cities are Nanjing, Chongqing, Guangzhou, Beijing, and Shenzhen. Apart from these representative companies, CSMS has several franchises across China, each dealing with a different product. These organisations also have, as part of their structure, a number of supporting functions, which support the different parts of the organisation in the areas of financial services, human resources and marketing. They all provide administrative services to the organisation as well as necessary support services to the other subsidiaries in China.

The problems

In the past few years, CSMS has suffered from its highest turnover rate of staff. There are several reasons that have contributed to this high turnover. The primary reason is considered to be the decision made by the company's headquarters in the United States to replace the managing director of the Chinese organisation. Although it is the right of the head office to replace its managers for whatever reasons it deems necessary, whether it is for promotion, poor performance or even personal reasons on the request of managers themselves, there are implications that may have undesirable consequences due to the different personalities and styles of the managers.

Different managing directors, obviously, have their own unique and different management styles. The previous managing director was sales-driven. The current managing director, however, tends to be more concerned with the differing systems operating within the organisation. His focus appears to be on developing a comprehensive managerial system for the Chinese operations. He has also placed a strong emphasis on legal issues within the company, a substantially greater focus as compared to the previous managing director. There are valid reasons, of course, for this change of focus.

The medical supply industry is a major player, world-wide, with a substantial earning capacity. The reason for the managing director's focus on legal compliance issues is due to the anti-corruption laws which are being emphasised in all of the subsidiaries, world-wide, of the organisation. The new managing director has put a comprehensive set of rules and regulations in place within the Chinese organisation to ensure compliance with the rules and policies of both the United States and China. This is obviously to protect the reputation of the company, but also to ensure that the company is not in danger of legal action being taken against it.

In addition, CSMS has also suffered from a stagnation in sales growth within the Chinese market. One reason for this is that a product that had been developed by them, that was up to date with new technology and current knowledge, gained increasing competition in the market. With the development of this new product, a patent protection was applied for, to ensure that the new product had a monopoly in the market. This new product was a big contributor to the total sales of the organisation. However, on the recent expiry of this patent, many competitors began to launch similar and lower-priced equivalent products. This was in direct competition with CSMS innovations that had required a substantial investment on their part. The introduction of competing products caused a great loss in the market share of CSMS. Due to the cheaper competition following the patent's expiry, and the other systems changes resulting from the appointment of the new managing director, there were a number of changes occurring in the corporate culture and in the management style of the company, as well as in the changes that had been introduced into the existing managerial system.

Many of the existing salespeople could not get used to the new style and culture of the organisation. This became the driving force for the departure of many of the salespeople within the organisation. Also, due to the new policies and management structure that had been implemented in the organisation, many of the salespeople felt that their previous autonomy to sell the product and to further promote CSMS had been limited. This resulted, therefore, in a loss of their income earning power and their freedom, by the imposition of a number of changed rules and policies that had to be followed by them. The result was an increase in turnover of the salespeople, many of them departing the organisation in a relatively short time-frame. The obvious outcome of these departures, of course, was a drop in the performance of the whole Chinese operation. The other financial impact was on training costs within the organisation, which substantially increased due to the urgent need to train new salespeople in organisational and product knowledge. Without this knowledge, inappropriate items might be sold to the customers, and if so, the reputation of the company could be damaged through bad publicity or other action. Furthermore, the high turnover rate tended to lower the morale of the employees remaining with the organisation, as they had lost the feeling of belonging to an extended family and instead tended to feel isolated and insecure, and the coordination of the sales teams suffered.

The solution

Ethical standards education

To try to increase morale and reduce turnover, the company placed greater emphasis on further educating the staff in the ethos of CSMS. One attempted solution that the organisation made to try to instil the philosophy of the organisation in the salespeople was to place more emphasis on the ethical issues existing within the organisation. As the company's reputation relies heavily on its ethical practices, this was considered to be a major focus that needed to be impressed on the staff.

One way that this ethical focus was attempted, was to sponsor a global ethical business course within the organisation. This was run through different key universities in China. Participants in the course normally had to attend the closest participating university for one weekend every month. The focus was on teaching these students how to align their own ethical standards to those of the organisation.

To further emphasise the ethical standards within the organisation, knowledge was disseminated throughout the organisation about the company's particular system of dealing with customers who may have complaints about their products. Within the company there was a grievance system put in place and this was mentioned to all the customers if they had a problem. Whenever they felt dissatisfied they could easily access the complaints department, also known as the Medical Affairs Department, of CSMS and express their concerns or problems. If it was found that the complaint of the customer was warranted, this department would try to resolve it at the local level if possible, but it would also report the problem to the Chinese Drug Administration Bureau. CSMS had a reputation for maintaining ethical standards in all countries in which it operated. As an example, a particular instance in the United States, in which the company withdrew its products from the market, even though the problem was caused, not by the company but by a third party, demonstrates the concern of the organisation for the well-being of its customers.

Staff motivation

In order to motivate their salespeople, a ranking system was introduced to determine effectively the sales performance of the employees. The performance of all the salespeople was checked every month, and the top 20 salespeople had their photographs published and posted throughout the company. This was considered by staff to be an honour, and for the salespeople to be praised for their efforts raised morale among the sales staff. If the salespeople successfully achieved, or exceeded, the sales quota for the month they received free domestic travel from the company as a bonus in appreciation of their efforts. Also, as CSMS was a sponsor of one of the nights at the 2008 Beijing Olympics, some of these salespeople were nominated to run in the torch relay as it went through the appropriate city in which the organisation's subsidiaries were located. Another incentive was free travel to Beijing to watch the Olympic Games, all expenses paid for the employee and his or her family.

The next motivational task was to rebuild the teams and a suitable team culture within the company. This was to try to foster increased team spirit and cooperation, not only among the individual staff members, but across the company. One method that was tried was to allow participation of all members of the team in coming to a decision about certain managerial matters within the company. This process provided some open form of consultation and gave the staff a feeling of ownership in a number of the decisions that were made. It also allowed the teams to adapt policies to suit their own individual circumstances.

Communication and accountability

The Chinese market was divided by the company into a number of territories. Each of these territories had a regional manager. In the past, none of these regional managers was held responsible for the actions or work of individual salespeople; they were only responsible for passing messages or communicating with the salespeople, and for the total amount of sales within their particular region. If the total sales reached or exceeded the quota, it was considered that performance was acceptable. The performance of the individual salesperson was not taken into account in this assessment; only the total of sales was monitored by the regional managers and the organisation.

New measures, however, ensured that each regional manager was required to mentor the salespeople in their particular territory. They were being held responsible for the performance of each of the salespeople within their particular region or zone. They were also responsible for providing training to them, especially in instances where performance had dropped below an accepted standard. Apart from performance, communication skills were also to be taught to the sales staff to assist them in improving their communication with the customer. The regional managers' performance was now directly related to the individual performance of each salesperson within the region. The evaluation of the performance of the regional salespeople and the regional manager was rewarded according to the performance of the region as well as that of the individual salesperson. Thus there was an incentive and responsibility for the regional managers to ensure that all members of the local staff were performing to an agreed level. This helped to strengthen the communication between the supervisor and his or her subordinate and also forced the supervisor to take an active role in assisting each of the salespeople. Performance bonuses were tied to the region and to the individual.

If the sales quota was exceeded and a very good result was achieved in the evaluation of the salespeople's performance, the opportunity was given to invite their major customers in the hospitals to attend an international conference abroad. The company, of course, would cover all the fees and costs of the medical practitioner customer. The employee, if he or she was considered to be an excellent and consistently high performer, also had the opportunity to be sent to the corporate headquarters of CSMS in the United States as a reward for their performance. There was also a possibility that they could be invited to work in another country for a set period of time, or be given additional training in the United States head office for one or two years.

Performance evaluation

Previously the performance of the salespeople was only evaluated either on a quarterly or yearly basis. The performance of the salespeople was now evaluated monthly, quarterly and yearly. Sometimes an evaluation took place every two weeks, especially if there were some issues that needed investigation. These brief evaluations were only to monitor the individual's performance if there was a problem, and to try to come up with solutions to the problem, allowing that it may not be related to the work of the employee but to external issues.

This initiative had positive aspects for the organisation, and helped to ensure the stability of the whole performance of the company. The down side was the additional pressure that was placed on the salespeople as a result of these more frequent assessments of their performance. Many of them felt that they were under scrutiny by the management. This regular assessment tended to be a contributing factor leading to the increased departure of salespeople within the organisation.

Orientation

For all new employees in the organisation, an orientation programme was introduced. All new employees from all over China are now sent to a series of training sessions in Shanghai and existing staff provide the new staff with suitable training on the company, its policies, procedures and culture. One member from each of the supporting staff groups participates in the programme and guides trainees on separate policies and procedures, such as how to place an order, how to reconcile costs, how to handle customers, how to handle complaints and how to comply with the anti-corruption law following head office policy. New employees are also made familiar with new business procedures within the company.

In addition to the joint training each individual receives supplementary training from their own business department. This is to make employees sufficiently familiar with the internal workings of the department to which they have been allocated.

The results

Some of the results of the measures introduced by the company to motivate the employees and reduce turnover did have a positive effect. Turnover of staff, especially the sales staff, was reduced. However, it was difficult to determine whether this was due to the measures that the company had adopted, or the expansion of the organisation and greater capital placed into product development. Another aspect was the changing economic climate at that particular time (2008). Whichever reason was responsible for the change in retention, the rate of staff turnover did reduce.

There are a number of possible ways to further reduce turnover within the company. Recruitment of a large number of new employees was considered, and sometimes if there were any vacancies existing at higher levels within the organisation, the company tried to recruit to these positions internally. This gave more career development opportunities to the current employees. If there was no success on internal recruitment processes, the company then recruited from external sources.

New external employee recruitment tended to come from two major sources. The first source of new employees came from campus recruitment exercises and the second source of recruitment was from the Chinese headquarter recruitment exercises. In these exercises the emphasis was placed on middle and senior management recruitment, for which there was considered to be no suitable internal candidate available. This, however, did point to a shortfall in the training programme, as no succession plan was fully functional to provide potential staff for the existing management roles when they became available.

Conclusion

As a result of the changes in management, many initiatives were introduced into the organisation's Chinese subsidiaries to reduce the drain of talented staff. The question to ask is: were the initiatives brought in too late, as many employees had already departed the company, taking with them valued corporate knowledge?

The initiatives, however, should assist in retaining staff in the future, especially through the more effective orientation programmes, although as mentioned above, a succession plan brought into alignment with the individual and group performance is possibly still needed, if not now, at least into the near future. Also, increased pressure to perform, while possibly desirable, could easily result in further staff losses if no adequate incentives are provided to the employees.

References

Bian Jianhui, (2005) 'Psychological contract and staff turnover', *Human Resource Development of China*, 6: 51–57.

Hu Yang, Liu Guohua and Xu Youlin (2007) 'Analysis and measures to staff turnover in time-based competition', *Human Resource Development of China*, 1: 38–41.

Liu Bing and Wang Hongxiao (2009) 'Turnover management of knowledge workers based on psychological contract', *Modern Management Science*, 9: 50–53.

Ma Xinjian (2004) 'Using compensation positioning strategy to control staff turnover', *Human Resource Development of China*, 11: 62–65.

Wang Liying, Ding Weiming and Ma Wanli (2004) 'An empirical study on knowledge worker turnover in hi-tech enterprises', *Science and Technology Management Research*, 4: 36–38.

Xu Ming (2007) 'A study on knowledge worker turnover in state-owned enterprises', *Human Resource Development of China*, 1: 45–48.

Zhang Jun (2009) 'Coping with crisis of sales force turnover', *Enterprise Management*, 7: 80–82.

Zhang Mingqin (2008) 'Study on key staff turnover factors in hi-tech enterprises', *Science and Technology Management Research*, 12: 372–373.

Zhang Qingyu and Jing Runtian (2006) 'Empirical study: factors influencing employee turnover in enterprises undergoing organizational changes', *Chinese Journal of Management*, 3(4): 482–487.

Zhang Yali and Yang Naiding (2009) 'Risk analysis and control on staff turnover', *Science of Science and Management of S. & T.*, 9: 42–44.

Zhao Ludan and Zhao Xinan (2004) 'The application of a new division method of psychological contract of human resources management in state-owned enterprises', *Science of Science and Management of S. & T.*, 11: 141–144.

Zhao Xiuwen (2009) 'Causing turnover of core staff in small and medium-sized enterprises and countermeasures', *Human Resource Development of China*, 2: 102–104.

Staff retention in the hotel industry

Introduction

This chapter examines a company in the hospitality industry, and raises a particular problem existing within that industry in China, and many other parts of the world. This is one of how to attract staff and ensure security of employment for those people, as well as providing them with a suitable salary to retain them in the business. Career paths are also a limiting feature of the hospitality industry, as the opportunity for promotion in the industry, especially in the smaller independent hotels, is extremely limited, compared to the larger hotel chains.

These problems result in minimal staff commitment and the view that the industry is only a stepping stone to a proper career, especially for younger college- or university-educated employees. Despite these problems, the hotel in this case study has developed a number of initiatives that at least demonstrate the potential for lateral thinking within the industry, to ensure the motivation and retention of employees.

Literature review

There has not been a substantial quantity of research undertaken in China to specifically study hotel staff turnover, apart from the acknowledgement that almost all research does mention the unusually high turnover rate in hotels in China as compared to many other industries. The average turnover rate in the hotel industry has been 23.95 per cent annually, from 1994 to 1999 (Li, 2008).

Some reasons for this high turnover rate have been suggested as being an unrealistic job preview causing disappointment among staff after they have been employed for a short period of time (Li, 2008), deficiencies in the HR system within the organisation and the management's attitudes (Li, 2008), including short-term oriented recruiting and inequities in the performance management system (You, 2009), insufficient training and development opportunities, non-competitive remuneration (You, 2009), and failure to provide necessary social security benefits (Li, 2008), such as sickness and retirement incentives.

Measures to reduce the turnover rate in hotels include emphasising work attitude and service consciousness (Jiao, 2007) as well as employee–organisation fit in recruiting (Shi, 2008), preparing detailed employment contracts (Jiao, 2007), offering job rotation and cross-training (Li, 2008; Jiao, 2007) not only in work-related skills, but also in the area of work ethics (You, 2009). Career planning (Li, 2008), challenging jobs, and diversified responsibilities (Li, 2005) are all effective ways to develop employees within the industry, but these appear to be lacking. Furthermore, a well-designed incentive system (Li, 2008; Shi, 2008; Zhou, 2006), which is strategy-consistent, balanced between internal and external equity, and performance-oriented to establish shared interest between the hotel and its core employees (You, 2009), improvement of the performance management system to ensure equity, flexibility and transparency (You, 2009; Shi, 2008), and expressing trust and respect (Shi, 2008; Zhou, 2005) through involving employees in the decision-making process and delegation to improve autonomy (Li, 2008; Shi, 2008; Li, 2005) have all been suggested as possible remedies to the turnover problem. In fact, delegation has been listed as one of the three most important factors to motivate knowledge-based employees in hotels (Li, 2005). Delegation will enable employees to make active and prompt responses to customer needs, which is essential for positive word-of-mouth for the hotel, where customers have one point of contact for decisions or answers to problems. This will enhance the employees' sense of accountability and will generate more input from them (Zhang, 2009). Apart from all of these aspects, a friendly working environment and positive culture (You, 2009; Jiao, 2007) is also important in increasing job satisfaction, which was found to be positively related to staff engagement in the hotel industry (Zeng and Zhao, 2009).

The organisation

Silver Hotel is a combined business and tourist hotel, located in Zhuhai, China. The normal source for employees for the hotel is from the local

Hotel School. It recently hired 20 new employees to work in the hotel in a range of functions. About 20 of the existing employees work in management roles, in the areas of administration, catering, reception and maintenance, among others.

The hotel commenced operations in 2007. It is a four-star hotel which has 130 rooms, ranging from standard to deluxe to small suites. Depending on the time of year, the hotel has a patronage of between 50 per cent and 80 per cent of its capacity. It has a number of restaurants, meeting rooms and conference rooms, as well as a beauty salon and a small art gallery, and tends to cater more for business people than for recreational visitors, although it is quite happy, obviously, to take holidaymakers; various recreational facilities are available as well as local tourist advice being provided. All rooms have internet access, which is viewed as an important incentive for business patronage.

The problems

There are five main problems, affecting Silver Hotel, and indeed China's service industry generally. The first one is the salary that is paid to staff, which is viewed as low compared to what may be offered in many other industries and in the higher rating hotels, although it is equivalent to other similar-sized hotels in the area. Many hotels work on a low profit margin, and as competition may be fierce, cost competitiveness is a factor that must be examined. Salary is an issue, but it may be used as an effective tool in retaining staff, if a guaranteed regular income could be maintained by the employees. The second problem, to which the salary component as a major contributing factor, is retaining staff within the industry, considering the other higher-paid opportunities that exist in many other industries. The third issue is that of corporate culture. How can staff affiliate with and embrace the corporate culture, work in assisting the company to meet its goals, follow the direction of the company and assist it in achieving its objectives? The fourth issue is the limited availability of promotional opportunities to employees within the hotel. A small company, such as a hotel, cannot provide a distinct career path for all employees, and as management opportunities are limited, there is minimal scope for promotion. The final issue is that of employment security. This tends to be dependent on the stability of the industry, which is susceptible to the fluctuations in the economy and the time of year, relating to vacancy rates.

These five problems are the major areas of concern to this hotel and its employees. Each of these will now be examined in more detail, with the first issue being that of remuneration and staff motivation.

Remuneration and motivation

Silver Hotel tends to compare the salaries paid to its employees with those paid to equivalent staff in hotels of a similar standard within the city and the region or province. This process is done through a benchmarking system to ensure that the company is competitive with those hotels of a similar ranking. Although the staff are comparatively well paid, they would probably say that for the work they do, they do not get sufficient money or other incentives. The hotel, however, considers that other benefits that it provides to the employee, apart from promotion and career path issues, comprise a very reasonable and attractive package. These benefits include job security, a staff canteen, and free trips for excellent employees. These are all part of the overall package that is given. Training, discussed below, is also provided, with the focus on the career development of the employees. Various social activities are provided to the staff to make them feel part of the extended family of the hotel. These allow the hotel to reward the commitment of the better employees working at the hotel. A hotel employee of the month programme is being considered for future implementation in an attempt to encourage some friendly competition, where employees may compete for an award. Although the award will not be an expensive one, it will allow employees to be proud of their achievements in the business.

Various training packages are provided to staff, which include training in such areas as ethics, human resource management and leadership skills, as well as various technical skills directly related to the employee's position within the organisation. These would cover topics such as how to serve customers correctly, new computer systems as applicable to the hotel, and maintenance of the hotel areas and grounds. If an employee shows potential to move into management, areas such as management and other development training related to the future managerial positions will be provided to them. Although a vacancy may not exist, the opportunity to fit into a position in the future is emphasised. Acting in a higher grade role can also be an incentive for an employee once appropriate training has been provided to that person.

Culture within the hotel

The role of culture within the hotel is to establish a shared vision within the organisation and to create some behavioural norms within the hotel environment. The mission of the hotel is to become the best business hotel in Zhuhai. The message sent across to the staff is to improve a little bit every day. This equates to continual improvement processes being incorporated into the hotel culture and of course means continually raising the target to be achieved by all employees. Feedback to recognise the efforts of staff to provide a better customer service or experience in the hotel is given by management through the performance management system.

This customer experience focus places emphasis on the employee to be detail-oriented. In other words, the management of the hotel requires that the staff focus on the little but important details that work to improve the customer service and perception of the hotel. These can be the cleanliness of the room, a follow-up call to determine if room service has been satisfactory, and even assistance to resolve a problem or re-book a flight if needed. The employees are empowered to have a sense of ownership of the guest's problems, and treat them as if they were their own.

This sense of ownership extends to other areas within the hotel, to do with the management and facilities provided. Employees have a mailbox in which they are encouraged to give their views and ideas about improvements that can be made to the hotel. They are also invited to give other ideas to management about the running of the hotel. If any of the suggestions that the employees make are adopted by management, the employee (or employees) who makes this suggestion is given a bonus as a result of that adoption. The size of the bonus may vary depending on the value and result of the suggestion, and it may not necessarily be a monetary award.

The management try to make employees feel as if they are part of an extended family within the hotel. As an example, if an employee is sick, the hotel will send another member of staff to assist in looking after the sick person if this is needed, or to visit them, if they are hospitalised. Although generally only a social call, it makes the employees feel as if they are a valued member of the hotel community, and that the company does care about their welfare. This approach helps to create and maintain a system of caring for the individual employees within the environment, which further enhances the family-focused atmosphere of the hotel. This can also work to make the employees feel less alone, and that they are a valued employee as well as a part of the larger hotel family.

Promotion and retention

As the hotel is only a small organisation, career paths for many of the employees may be limited. One thing that the hotel is looking at is expansion, to open up or take over other hotels in the area and throughout China (realising that this will be a long-term plan). To further this goal, the hotel wishes all of its staff to incorporate certain core competencies. It is then hoped that the learning of these core competencies will allow the employees to operate in a larger environment, and enable the company to create more opportunities for promotion. Management also believe that this would enable the business to gain a competitive advantage over its competition. Examples of the core competencies that the hotel would like all of the employees to have include team-building skills, technical skills, marketing skills, communication skills and people management skills. Although they realise that not all employees can attain all of these skills, they consider that a spread of competency is needed for the proposed expansion. As a result of this, they are training selected staff members.

To assist in employees obtaining some of these skills and to identify possible gaps in the level of knowledge of their staff, job rotation with appropriate training is also provided to prevent them from becoming bored with doing one role on a continual basis. This is optional, and staff do have a right to decline any new placement if they wish, as some staff may prefer to remain doing the one job, but if accepted, this allows them the variety to extend their knowledge of the hotel and the business, as well as becoming more valuable to the organisation. This is especially important in instances of employee departure, which could result in a shortage of a particular necessary skill for the hotel. This enables a multi-skilled employee to be slotted into other positions as required, while working to build an automatic succession plan.

To assist in motivating staff, good leadership skills and communication tend to be important abilities used by the hotel management. Bonuses, plus praise of the employees, are the most commonly used tool to motivate staff, although management do realise the limitations of this. Also, promotion, or training to allow a staff member to be promoted into management, can be used as an effective tool to motivate high performers.

Another tool that is used by the hotel management is to take employees on external activities, not related to the business, with their families outside of the hotel. These may include barbeques or picnics, or other social and sporting activities. This can work to make the employees' families appreciate the organisation and value the work that their partners and parents do on a daily basis.

Staff turnover

Although the hotel tries its best to retain staff by using a number of the initiatives mentioned above, staff turnover is still reasonably high. The majority of staff turnover tends to be in the first line of employment, which is the entry phase for most of the new staff. For example, in some departments within the hotel, such as those staff who prepare the rooms, staff turnover could be as high as 100 per cent over a twelve-month period. This rate of turnover is not that unusual for hotels and similar service industries, but it is still an unacceptable rate.

There appears to be no single reason for this high turnover of staff. One reason could be the culture of the hotel, as it is relatively new and is hiring many new employees to work for it. This implies that the hotel currently does not have a very mature culture. However, this culture can be developed, which is possibly easier to do than to change an old culture that has been in place for many years.

At the management level, some line managers, because they are paid a rate similar to many at a similar position in other hotels, may become bored with working in the same organisation and look for a fresh establishment to work for. This could be because they lack challenge and variety in their position.

Another reason is that, as the company is newly established, it requires a large number of new employees to work for it. Those employees tend not to have much experience working within the industry. They may not have the proper or formal qualifications, and may consider themselves underqualified, so, therefore, lack confidence to work in that job. This may make them look for another position in another company at a different level that they feel matches their skills, despite the training that they were given when commencing at the hotel.

Other incentives

Apart from salary and sick pay, the hotel does provide other incentives to its employees. These include a monthly bonus if the employee reaches a target that is mutually set between the employee and the management through the staff appraisal process. There is also a yearly target set for the employees and if this target is achieved, they are then provided with an additional bonus for the year. If both the monthly and yearly targets are achieved this can provide a substantial bonus at the end of the year to the employees. It is a form of continuous performance appraisal or assessment that is done on a monthly and yearly basis.

Conclusion

This study examined a number of problems that also exist in many hotel and similar service industries in China. Many staff consider that the service industry is only a part-time job, and will look for other positions in other areas. In China, as with other countries, similar problems are being faced in this industry as a stronger focus is being placed on service and hospitality in the developing economy.

The reasons for some of these problems have been highlighted in the case study. Many employees view the remuneration as insufficient, while others think that a career path in the industry is lacking. Although training is given, this perception still remains. The organisation is attempting to build a culture which will lead to growth, but it remains to be seen if these efforts succeed and staff turnover, not only in the lower ranks in the organisation, but also at the higher management level, reduces.

References

Jiao Yonghui (2007) 'Intern management in Singapore Conrad Hotel', *Human Resource Development of China*, 9: 89–91.

Li Changyan (2005) 'Motivation of knowledge-based employees in hotels', *Contemporary Manager*, 14: 132–133.

Li Yanyan (2008) 'How to improve the situation of high staff turnover in hotels', *Economic Forum*, 23: 100–101.

Shi Weijun (2008) 'Soft management in hotels', *Management and Administration*, 8: 50–51.

You Fuxiang (2009) 'Analysis of turnover factors of core employees in hotels', *Human Resource Development of China*, 4: 105–107.

Zeng Hui and Zhao Liming (2009) 'Employee engagement and service performance in hotel industry', *Journal of Beijing Technology and Business University (Social Science)*, 24(4): 96–100.

Zhang Liqin (2009) 'Methods and techniques for hotel employee delegation', *Reform and Opening*, **12**: 105–106.

Zhou Jianfeng (2006) 'Establish mutual loyalty to retain high-achievers – the application of ERG theory in hotel management', *Contemporary Manager*, **1**: 110–111.

Human resource problems in a high-tech business incubator

Introduction

This chapter is concerned with the development of small and medium size businesses in smaller cities in China. Although many people when they think of industry and commerce in China think of Shanghai and related cities, many smaller cities in other areas of China are also experiencing strong growth, with the potential to grow further as resources become available.

The most valuable, and surprisingly scarce, resource in China is suitably qualified staff that are needed to allow these industries to grow and contribute to the dynamic Chinese economy. To assist these fledgling industries, many cities have set up business incubators, to provide companies with the basic support and resources needed. Unfortunately, these organisations still have difficulty in obtaining the appropriately-qualified people needed for their operation.

This case study examines a number of initiatives that are being used to recruit both new employees and population to a coastal city and its surrounding areas, not only to cater for current growth, but also to provide future opportunities in the area. Special zones such as this are viewed as a way of providing employment to an area, improving the level of education and further developing workforce skills and abilities, thus raising the economic standing, not only of the city, but of the province and of China generally.

Literature review

In China, business incubators are generally operated by three types of organisations, namely, government bodies, private corporations, and universities and other research institutions (Li et al., 2005; Yin, 2008). These incubators generally serve two purposes. From the macro aspect, incubators help to promote regional economies (Li et al., 2005) by fostering industrial clusters (Zhang, 2007). From the micro aspect, incubators normally provide financing, marketing, consulting, legal, staff training services and support, and opportunities for exchange with businesses outside the incubator (Liu and Zhang, 2003; Li et al., 2005; Zhang, 2007). Particular evidence has been given to demonstrate the boosting effect that science and technology business incubators in Wuhan (which is located in central China) have had on the rapid development of the whole region (Huang et al., 2006). More general effects of the positive impact of the incubators have been discussed by Li and Zhang (2009).

Frequently, though, it is the local area government and the management committee from the development zone that oversee the operations of the high-tech areas. This commitment by the government is essential if an incubator programme is to work successfully, as well as to assist in the development and growth of a regional economy, through attracting more industry to the area, which assists job and population growth (Lalkaka, 2003; Nolan, 2003).

Research on business incubators in China is mainly focused on the development of the business incubators and venture capital, the effectiveness of business incubator operations in China, the role of the government in their development, and other miscellaneous issues encountered during the development of these incubators (Yin, 2008). Only a very limited number of articles from the literature discuss human resources issues separately. To enhance HR services, business incubators may cooperate with various professional training institutions to provide training services, maintain close contact with employment agencies at different levels to ensure the availability of qualified candidates to companies in the incubators, and maintain good relationships with relevant government bodies to attract overseas professionals and investments (Zhang et al., 2009). Other possible suggestions include establishing national or regional incubator alliances to promote information exchanges and to enhance the incubators' negotiating power with external institutions, constructing networks among enterprises within the incubator and creating a positive incubator culture (Zhong, 2003).

The performance of a business incubator can be evaluated through measuring its capacity to provide infrastructure, governmental services, financing, technical support, management support, employment services and information services (Xiong and Fang, 2009). Evaluation criteria for soft services provided by business incubators are stability, convenience, professionalism and comprehensiveness, as well as confidentiality in instances where publicity or leaked information of a new initiative may lead to loss of investment, or security breaches (Sun, 2003). An empirical study conducted among entrepreneurs and managerial staff in 25 business incubators in several coastal cities suggested that financing services and information intermediary services should be the core provisions of incubators. Another aspect of note is the need to exert a significant positive effect on the comprehensive performance of incubators. However, their current financing services can hardly satisfy the needs of the enterprises that request it, due to the shortage of capital (Zhang and Xing, 2006).

The acknowledgement of a good human resources plan, however, tends to be missing in many of these incubators. 'Without a human resource management mechanism in place, Chinese high-tech enterprises (may) confront many problems. Fast, stable development will only be possible if Chinese high-tech enterprises establish (effective) human resource management systems' (Zhao and Yang, 2008: 26–27). To encourage innovation and develop new industries, a high-tech incubator requires this high level of human resource skills to lead the way in both technology and economic advancement (Müller and Etzkowitz, 2000). Chan and Lau (2004) found nine criteria that could lead to a successful incubator programme. These were pooling resources, sharing resources, consulting services, a public image, networking advantages, clustering effect, geographic proximity, cost subsidies and funding support.

Support services to the staff working in the incubator are also a factor that needs to be accounted for (Sun, Wenbin and Leung, 2007). Without this support the programmes may have minimal success in their implementation. In the case study below, efforts of both the local government and the business park management are working to look after the needs of both the staff working in the business park and the anticipated needs that are required to attract people to the area to work in the various companies supported by the incubator.

The organisation

Southern Coast Region High-Tech Business Incubator has as its aim, to provide technical, administrative, legal and other support services to small and medium start-up enterprises in the region. The main mission of the incubator is to foster an environment which will assist these new start-up companies to develop further and become larger and more profitable over time, with the hope of bringing in more new business to the region. The incubator has four broad goals.

The first is to provide, or assist in providing, finances for the fledgling organisations in the area to develop and grow. This can extend to providing small loans to the enterprise, but if the money required is beyond certain limitations, it may then locate other sources that are willing to provide these funds, and in certain circumstances, may act as a guarantor to the lending institution.

The second goal is to provide human resources support services to the company. For example, it is sometimes difficult to find technical or senior management people to work in these enterprises and it is the role of the HR department to assist in searching for and providing suitable people to work in these different businesses. The priority is to source local staff but it also extends to searching for staff in other areas of China.

The third goal is to assist the organisation in developing policies that meet its requirements and those of any governing authority that has an impact on it. The problem with many small organisations is that they are not familiar with the various rules and regulations that are required by law for them to operate effectively. So the third goal is to make the new organisation knowledgeable of these requirements and to assist in writing policies and procedures to allow the organisations to run legally. A part of this process is to assist the organisations to register and apply for any patents if required. This will then protect the business incubator but more importantly would protect the new enterprise.

The fourth goal is to assist in providing marketing expertise to the new enterprises. Many new enterprises are not familiar with the role that marketing may play in promoting their business. Therefore the incubator insists on providing this necessary marketing and promotional expertise to the company, realising that without proper promotion, potential customers may not be aware of the product or services offered.

The business incubator services approximately 85 enterprises in its immediate environment, by providing all of the support services that are thought to be necessary for the new start-up companies. The business incubator supports many companies located within the incubator park itself, but it also supports the high-tech industrial park environment generally, thus expanding its responsibility into these other areas. In the broader areas, the supporting function can potentially assist up to a thousand small businesses in many of their needs.

Compared to many other countries, a small business in China is not classified as a small business based on the number of employees that are working for it. The classification is based on the monetary turn-over that the company experiences in a twelve-month period. For example, a medium-sized enterprise may have a turnover of approximately 50 million RMB per year. So although a company may have only a small number of employees, it will be classified, not based on the staffing figure, but on the financial success of the enterprise.

The problems

Popular views of the city and a general problem

The major problem in the city, similar to other small cities in China, is finding adequate numbers of professional staff to service the growing operations of many of the companies. A lack of staff can work to inhibit growth of these start-up enterprises, and has the potential to lead to their failure, despite many of the good initiatives that are being developed, which can lead to positive outcomes for the country. This then leads into the possibility of enticing employees from other areas. It is thus becoming quite common, when searching for these suitable staff, that employers may have to look for employees in other major and minor cities outside the immediate region. This search for staff may also extend to looking for employees in other distant and remote areas of China.

In general, this problem is not unique to this city. The staffing issue is one of the biggest problems that incubators in China generally face and is not only a problem when an organisation is looking for professional or technical staff. It exists at all levels, from labouring staff to professional and managerial employees, as well as technical staff.

In this particular city, however, the issue tends to be of more of an historical nature. It is only since 1988 that the city has had its classification changed from a village to a city. This means that there may not be a large candidate pool as the city is still expanding, but the perception to view it as a village still remains strong. It also leads to the perception by potential employees that, even though the city is growing, it is not only small in size, but does not offer the opportunities that the larger cities, such as Shanghai or Guangzhou, are able to offer. These opportunities include salary, career progression and a larger number of organisations with more potential, even though the city does have many other benefits that the larger metropolises do not have, one major aspect being quality of life.

The solution

In an attempt to resolve the staffing and related population issues, industry and the provincial government explored two initiatives. The first that was considered was not an immediate solution but had future implications. The government and industry looked at securing the education of future employees by encouraging students to come and enrol in the universities in this city and to undertake job-related training. It was believed more likely that the students, on completion of their studies, would stay there if suitable employment was available. The second initiative was just generally attracting people to the city and region from other larger areas or cities within China.

The time taken to develop new talent is the problem with the first initiative, although it does indicate a longer-term vision of staff training and attraction. Even though the efforts and initiatives being used are currently attracting more people to work in this city, due to the efforts of the local government and businesses, the time taken for the universities and other educational colleges to further develop and train these people may take a number of years before a sufficient pool of staff are available to work in these many companies. However, they are hopeful that over time, sufficient staff will be available to resource these myriad companies that are developing in the high-tech incubator.

The municipal government is also hoping to attract more universities in China to set up campuses in the city. Apart from servicing the local population as it grows, it is hoped that the new campuses, many of them from major universities in China, will also attract more students from other parts of the country to come and study in the city. This will then directly provide additional labour to the town as the students graduate and learn of the potential opportunities available to them, as well as the better living environment as compared to many of the larger cities in China.

As an additional training resource, the local government has also set up its own professional training centre to develop new talent in the area. Its main role is to offer short courses to equip the students with skills that will make them more attractive to business. It is aimed more at mature workers who are living in that area as compared to attracting new graduates. There are obvious financial and social reasons for this approach.

Financially, it is cheaper to train local residents as it saves any cost in re-locating people to the region. These people are also more dedicated to staying in the city due to family reasons, as compared to other people migrating to the city, with the strong possibility that they may leave once marketable skills have been obtained. Socially, it avoids the possibility of creating an 'underclass' within the area, consisting of low-skilled, low-paid employees. The opportunity is also available for these residents to increase their qualifications further due to the push to attract other institutions to set up facilities in the region. The incubator has been instrumental in providing the attraction for higher-learning organisations to consider opening.

The incubator, in its further search for talent, has also been approaching many of the inland universities that are located in areas where jobs are not as plentiful, with higher unemployment due to a lack of industry to absorb these graduates. The source of many of these graduates is from other less developed provinces located inland in China. However, in this region, as in the rest of China, there are a large number of multinational companies as well as local businesses competing for these talented people. With the shortage of suitable talent in many parts of China, competition can be fierce for these students. It does have, though, a geographic advantage (being on the coast) as well as other attractions that may suit younger families.

Compared to many of the inland cities and the larger coastal cities, the local government is marketing itself as a young city with multiple and fresh job opportunities, due to the range of small industries, and this potential may suit the younger graduates. They are also placing an emphasis on the opportunities that are available for development and promotion. This is emphasised by the start-up opportunities and the ability to get in to many of these companies at ground level. However, compared to many of the other major cities located on the coastal fringe, the region, to a younger person, may seem a less attractive option, lacking the glamour and attraction of cities such as Shanghai. What the local government of the city can do, however, is to provide some more attractive policies that may appeal to younger people, as well as providing some tax incentives to make it easier to bring potential employees to the area.

There are a number of incentives that the government is making available to graduates coming from other provinces. Where it can be potentially difficult to move from one province to another due to restrictions placed on migration by the government, one incentive is the status given to new employees to allow them to become residents of the city. In China if you try to transfer your residence from one city to another or from one province to another, you have to pay a fee to the government. The local government will assist in skilled migration by paying this fee on behalf of the new resident. It should be noted, however, that there is evidence of a relaxing of this migration policy.

A second aspect is the advantage of living there compared to living inland in China, with the comparative advantage of living near the sea and having a better and more temperate climate. This environmental advantage can be of benefit, especially if there is a young family concerned, as the coastal city lacks the pace of the larger cities and has a more relaxed lifestyle.

The third advantage is the income tax privileges that are given to the individual employee. In China if your income exceeds a certain level you have to pay a higher rate of tax. However, in this city they have increased the level of income that needs to be earned before an employee is required to pay taxes. This allows employees to earn a larger salary while paying a lower rate of tax, as compared to other larger cities which have higher taxation rates.

These joint government–incubator solutions have tended to have some impact on the success of the incubator and the young companies that are hoping to lead China further towards becoming a highly-developed nation. However, the similar push by other regions may increase competition for valued, skilled staff, and it remains to be seen whether the region can maintain its momentum of development.

Conclusion

As noted above, a number of initiatives have been developed to entice staff to come to the city to work in the business park incubator, thus assisting its growth as well as the growth of the city. These initiatives have been a result of a combined effort by the local government and the management of the business park. As to the success of these initiatives, it is still unclear, but early indicators point to an increase in migration to the city.

The development of university campuses can be viewed as a long term strategy, which will provide a continuous stream of graduates to the city. It is hoped that many of these graduates will remain and work in that environment, although the pull of the larger cities does pose a danger to the retention of some members of the population in this region. It does show potential, however, and with the investment of the universities in the city, it is apparent that these educational organisations also see the city as a growing entity.

The incentives given by the government also are potentially beneficial. The lower taxation rate coupled with the payment of immigration fees can work to remove some of the financial concerns of new citizens. Finally, the advantage of a better living environment, though hard to quantify, can be viewed as a valuable enticement as China realises the value of its natural resources.

References

Chan, K., and Lau, T. (2004) 'Assessing technology incubator programs in the science park: the good, the bad and the ugly', *Technovation*, 25(10): 1215–28.

Huang Tao, Li Guang and Mei Shihong (2006) 'The scientific enterprise incubator and the growing-up of Central China', *Science of Science and Management of S&T*, 11: 58–61.

Lalkaka, R., (2003) 'Business incubators in developing countries: characteristics and performance', *International Journal of Entrepreneurship and Innovation Management*, 3(1/2): 31.

Li Daisong, Wang Ruidan and Ma Xin (2005) 'A study on the characterisitc of incubator industry and operation models of Chinese business incubators', *Science Research Management*, 26(3): 8–11.

Li Juheng and Zhang Meiling (2009) 'The practical logic of science and technology business incubator (STBI) in promoting regional harmonious development', *Forum on Science and Technology in China*, 2(2): 58–61.

Liu Ke and Zhang Ping (2003) 'Research on the development mode of incubator of technology enterprise', *Science and Technology Management Research*, 6: 42–4.

Müller, K., and Etzkowitz, H. (2000) 'Comparative advantage: S & T human resources: the comparative advantage of the post-socialist countries', *Science and Public Policy*, 27(4): 285–91.

Nolan, A., (2003) 'Public policy on business incubators: an OECD perspective', *International Journal of Entrepreneurship and Innovation Management*, 3(1.2): 22–30.

Shuming Zhao and Huifang Yang (2008) 'Management practices in high-tech environments and enterprises in the People's Republic of China', *The Chinese Economy*, 41(3): 17–33

Sun, H., Wenbin, N. and Leung, J. (2007) 'Critical success factors for technological incubation: case study of Hong Kong science and technology parks; *International Journal of Management*, 24(2): 346–63.

Sun Weiye (2003) 'Service package of S&T business incubator and evaluation', *Science of Science and Management of S&T*, 24(3): 87–9.

Xiong Shengxu and Fang Xiaobo (2009) 'A study on service capacity of S&T business incubators in China', *Economic Forum*, 4(7): 42–6.

Yin Qun (2008) 'A survey on research hotspots of the business incubator', *Science Research Management*, 29(1): 157–63.

Zhang Wei and Xing Xiao (2006) 'An empirical research on the relationship between service project and service performance in technology business incubator', *Science of Science and Management of S&T*, 4: 159–64.

Zhang Yuqi, Liu Aijun and Wan Qi (2009) 'A tentative study on service capacity construction of S&T incubators: a case of National University S&T Park in Nanjing', *Science and Technology Management Research*, 11: 79–82.

Zhang Zhenyu (2007) 'Thought on the business incubator's function of accelerating enterprises' growth', *Scientific Management Research*, 25(2): 38–40.

Zhao, S. and Yang, H. (2008) 'Management practices in high-tech environments and enterprises in the People's Republic of China', *Chinese Economy*, 41(3): 17–33.

Zhong Weidong (2003) 'Thinking about restructuring the operational system of S&T business incubators', *Forum on Science and Technology in China*, 11(6): 61–6.

Staff retention, motivation and commitment at the China Electrical Components organisation

Introduction

High staff turnover is a major problem in Chinese organisations, especially in the fast-developing eastern regions of the country, with staff changing jobs and careers for a variety of reasons. This is occurring increasingly in the Chinese environment and can be a great cost to a company, with recruitment and training forming a major expense. To keep staff motivated and happy increasingly requires not only financial incentives, but a caring and family approach to the workforce, as well as pleasant and equal conditions of employment. These aspects tend to mean more to employees than money, although this is not to discount the motivational factor of increased compensation.

The China Electrical Components (CEC) organisation is a family-owned and operated company which has managed to maintain a low turnover of staff through its establishment of good facilities and a family environment. Employees are embedded in the culture of the company and as a reward, there are many opportunities given to staff. This, in turn, tends to be a motivational factor in staff retention, leading to increased training opportunities and a strong commitment to the organisation.

Literature review

To reduce staff turnover and become an organisation of choice, effective and charismatic leadership is deemed to be essential. Howell and Shamir

(2005) studied the under-researched field of charismatic, inspirational or transformational leadership and the role of these leaders in inspiring staff and developing better relationships with their 'followers'. They also considered that a collectivist culture (such as China) is more likely to follow this style of leadership than an individualistic culture.

Research by Babcock-Roberson and Strickland (2010) found a significant positive relationship between charismatic leadership and work engagement, which in turn was significantly positively related to organisational commitment behaviour. So if a charismatic manager is in charge of an organisation, it is possible that this characteristic will filter to supervisors and in turn the average employee, with a strong focus on workplace engagement. So if an organisation can ensure that staff are committed to their immediate supervisor, this will in turn result in benefits to the organisation and positive performance outcomes with good relationships occurring among staff and management (Landry et al., 2010)

Hui et al. (2004) considered that a relationship between the psychological contract and organisational commitment can be as applicable in the Chinese context as in the Western context. Due to the relationships that can be developed between management and employee, suitable behaviour (which may include retention in the job) tends to be positive. The commitment and experiences they have with their employer can relate to the commitment that an employee devotes to his or her employer (Organ, 1990).

This commitment can take a number of forms. If employees are engaged in their work and have sufficient resources (which may include intrinsic and extrinsic motivators, job autonomy, and equity), an organisation is more likely to retain its staff. Also if opportunities are given to staff to learn and promote, engagement within the organisation can increase (De Lange et al., 2008).

Engagement can also be linked to the three component models of commitment (affective, normative and continuance). When examining this model it could be argued that affective commitment, or emotional attachment to the company, and normative commitment, the feeling of obligation to remain, are more likely to be the reasons for low turnover and improved staff motivation. However, in the cultural context, affective commitment could be considered to be the better predictor of positive organisational outcomes (Yu and Egri, 2005). The experiences that the employees have at the workplace can then be linked to the commitment that develops (Allen and Meyer, 1990). This could be taken further to the supervisors' roles in which they themselves have a similar commitment.

The organisation

China Electrical Components (CEC) is a leading player in the low-voltage electrical power transmission and distribution industry in China. Its sales turnover reached in excess of 2 billion RMB by the end of 2006. It was also ranked 15th in the list of the top 100 Chinese companies released by Forbes, which evaluated all private companies with or without public listings in China. CEC was classified as the leading organisation in the power transmission and distribution and controlling devices sector in the China machinery summit. CEC was also nominated as the best-known national trademark, one of the most prestigious honours for outstanding enterprises, by the China State Administration body for industry and commerce.

The company was founded in 1984 in Wenzhou. In the last 22 years, CEC has expanded from a home-based workshop of seven workers to a leading manufacturer of electrical products, with eight specialised branches, over 800 specialised partners and with more than 16,000 employees. The main product lines of CEC cover the following categories: high, medium and low voltage electrical apparatus, power transmission and distribution equipments, measuring meters and instruments, electrical products for construction, automation control devices and automobile applications.

The problems

From the time CEC was established it was purely a family-owned company, with the shareholders being family members of the founder. However, as this company has progressed and grown over the years, it has faced increased competition due to the higher demand for goods as a result of the developing economy. In 2005 and 2006, many problems were encountered. With the entry of China into the World Trade Organization, many foreign companies entered the Chinese market, thus giving CEC increased competition domestically. As well as multinational enterprises entering the Chinese market, there have also been a number of takeover bids for many Chinese-owned organisations, due to the opening of the Chinese economy to a more free-market approach. As a result CEC had to undertake an expansion plan itself, to maintain its market share in China. This involved increasing the number of factories and training staff in new skills, as well as marketing its product range more effectively. Better ways to manage staff and reduce turnover were also needed, as the owners of the organisation realised that these were creating additional but unnecessary costs to the company.

Concurrently there were also a great number of entrants into the industry in which it was a manufacturer. Additionally, apart from the pressure caused by the entrance into the Chinese market of many foreign competitors, the price of copper, which was CEC's prime raw material, began to soar. This increase in price posed many problems for the effective operation of the company. To try to eliminate, or at least reduce, these, the company decided that a number of changes had to be made to its internal structure.

The solutions

As a result of the above challenges, in 2006 the company produced a new strategic plan called the 'Phoenix Rising.' Like the Phoenix, a mythical bird that was created (or recreated) from the ashes, the organisation itself would rise up from the problems it was facing, and become a better company as a result of tackling and resolving these matters. The implication for the organisation was that it had suffered many great disadvantages but that it would regain its advantage by renewing itself through the restructuring.

Initial action was to make a number of changes to the style of management within the organisation. The management style and operations were outmoded and not applicable to the new challenges facing the company. A family style of management was not necessarily the most appropriate in changing conditions. The managerial philosophy, style and approaches were therefore updated by forming a relationship with another company.

The first stage of this approach was engaging in a joint venture with a multinational electric component manufacturer. This company was used as a mentor and trainer through which CEC was hoping to learn the managerial style, philosophy and approach of a multinational enterprise, and then to transfer this knowledge, with modification as an acknowledgement to the prevailing culture, across to the Chinese organisation.

A major change that was introduced involved removing many of the previous major (family) shareholders of CEC from managerial positions and replacing them with professional managers. These managers were recruited from other organisations, and as an incentive to encourage them to join CEC and to participate in the re-building of the organisation, a number of share options were given to them. This process was called 'equity dilution', where the ownership was not only in the hands of the family, but shared among other staff. The new managers were cherry-picked to bring either technical knowledge or professional management expertise to the organisation. Strict criteria were used in deciding how to select and recruit them for the organisation. CEC wanted to endow them with a high level of empowerment and authority to enable them to effectively manage the organisation without the need to refer to the owners for advice. Thus, the managers were effectively given the power to manage.

When many companies in China hire new managers, they tend to give them the title of Vice President within the organisation. The decision was made, at CEC, to give the title of President to these new managers to demonstrate the high level of empowerment and authority that was being given to them. However, prior to their final appointment, to ensure that they did fit in with the culture of the organisation, there was a probationary period so that they could learn the culture and the operations of CEC. They initially came in, therefore, as department heads to ensure that they had some contact with the corporate strategy of the company. This tended to give them sufficient time to come to know their employees and to learn how to cooperate with them. Concurrently this also allowed the employees to become familiar with the management style of the new managers. After a manager had been with the organisation for some time and was becoming familiar with the staff and the operations, the board then met to decide if the person was a suitable fit within the organisation. If the person could pass this probationary period the decision was then made as to the level within the organisation at which they would be appointed, as well as their major responsibilities.

As a result of the success of this initiative to employ new management talent, professional managers now occupy many of the key positions within the organisation. Some examples of the key positions held by the professional managers include the legal director position and the financial director. Coupled with this promotion or positioning of new employees, the company also offered a very good training system for all its staff. This training system allowed them to be promoted to vacancies as they occurred if they demonstrated the correct aptitude, skills and abilities. It was not only available to the managers, but to all technical, sales and other staff within the company. Sourcing suitable staff to be trained for possible promotion was part of the recruitment and appraisal process.

As an example of this process, there were two sources of people that were employed in the sales and marketing areas. One option was to recruit internally from CEC's existing staff members. The first point of contact was the front-line of workers within the organisation, where they were observed and appraised, and a decision made as to whether they had the potential to promote into higher positions, especially in the sales area. The benefit of this internal sourcing was familiarity with the products of CEC, as well as having an appreciation of the internal culture and operations of the company. This familiarity enabled the employees, once promoted to a sales position, to more actively demonstrate to potential buyers the value, quality and follow-up service that was available to the customer.

The other source of new employees was fresh graduates coming from the Chinese education system. Graduates are recruited directly from universities into sales and management trainee positions. As part of the training programme for graduates, these new employees had to work with the front-line workers for a period of three to twelve months, to enable them to fully understand the product lines and the operations of the organisation. This training programme enabled the fresh graduates to become familiar with the assembly lines, the manufacturing of the product and also the supply chain within the organisation. A job rotation process was also introduced to enable all workers within the company, especially these new staff members coming from universities and colleges, to become familiar with the total operation of the organisation.

The next major issue was ensuring that there were sufficient funds for growth and expansion of the organisation. Before 2005 the organisation had had no difficulty in gaining new finance. Since then, however, due to the entry of foreign competition, they found that it was becoming increasingly difficult to obtain new funding for expansion. Many of the new entry foreign enterprises were transnational corporations with multiple branches in many countries. The advantage that these organisations had was that they could utilise their resources at the global level instead of relying on the small financial impact of the Chinese investors. It was therefore difficult for CEC to solve their financing problem, compared to the lack of difficulty that the multinational enterprises had in gaining finance for their operations. One way that was sought to resolve this problem was for the organisation to float on both the Chinese stock market and the American market, NASDAQ, to gain sufficient funding to allow the organisation to increase its growth and expansion.

The morale and motivation of staff

A positive aspect of CEC was that it enjoyed a very low staff turnover rate, due to the culture and the benefits that the company provided to all of the workers. This is contrary to many private organisations in China, which suffer from high turnover due to the salary, working conditions and environment offered by some companies.

There are several reasons for low staff turnover at CEC. The main reason is the role that the owner and director played in making CEC a friendly and good place to work. The role of the owner and director is viewed as a very important element in maintaining staff dedication and morale within the company. The personal leadership style and charisma of the owner in particular played a big role in reducing and minimising staff turnover. This tended to build confidence in all the staff working below him within the organisation. The owner had the rare ability to convey his vision to all workers within the organisation, and as a result they tended to share this vision, effectively bringing staff into alignment with his goals. He also held a very broad view of staff abilities, giving opportunities for all workers to perform and excel in their chosen tasks. Poor performers were provided with training and also given other opportunities to improve themselves, so they could meet the required standards of the company. Additionally, as mentioned above, a career development path, or the prospect of career development with a subsequent promotion, was given to all employees who displayed the initiative and ability to expand their knowledge and skills.

As an example, it was not uncommon for front-line workers to be promoted rapidly to a level more suited to their abilities, and there have been instances of front-line workers, on entering the company, gaining promotion to the position of vice president, as well as other similar executive roles, such as assistant to the president of the company. The ability to promote within the organisation someone who only had a junior high school certificate to the level of vice president demonstrated to all employees the potential career paths that were open to them if they displayed the correct attitude, aptitude and ability.

Another reason for the devotion of staff to the organisation was that the management style was very humane, and was inclusive of all employees. In other words, it was very people-focused. A paternalistic attitude by senior management tended to be behind this caring approach, where all employees felt that they were part of the family of the company. There was ample opportunity for communication on a two-way basis within the company, as well as a job rotation plan to allow employees to experience other departments and understand the problems that each particular department faced in the day to day operations. Treatment of the staff was considerate of their own family issues as well, possibly due to the strong family ownership that had existed from when the organisation was smaller. As an example of this sympathetic treatment, one employee was separated from his wife for work reasons, the employee working in the Wenzhou factory, and his wife working in the Beijing office. On becoming aware of this problem, at the first available vacancy, the manager provided a transfer of this employee to the Beijing office of CEC to allow the family to be reunited.

Another aspect of the motivational culture that existed within the organisation was the benefits that the company gave to its employees. Within private enterprises in Wenzhou province where CEC was located, very few of these companies gave a high level of medical and accident insurance to employees. CEC was the first company in Wenzhou province to ensure that all employees, including front-line employees, had full insurance coverage, to protect them from any unforeseen occurrences. Apart from this, an extremely good working environment was also provided to the employees. The owner of the organisation considered that a good working environment was essential to get the optimum output from staff, as well as ensuring the satisfaction of employees. Whereever a plant was built by the organisation, a very openplan style and park environment was provided. Employees were offered suitable recreation facilities, good training classrooms, as well as provision of water features to relax them when on a break. Although this was an extra expense to the company when building its facilities, the manager thought it was worth it as it improved the working conditions and lifestyle of the company, allowing all employees to work in a more relaxing and meaningful environment. Management viewed that these facilities motivated all its employees, allowing them to work both harder and better.

An issue of particular note was the payment structure given to the employees. The level of payment, for example, for the managers was spread over an A, B, and C payment system. The salary across these three levels varied greatly, from 200,000 RMB to 500,000 RMB per annum. This demonstrated a big differential between the levels of salary available to managers within the company. A broadband remuneration system was offered to all of the employees. This salary arrangement was a good motivator to staff, by demonstrating that if they worked hard and improved their performance, they would be suitably rewarded by a substantial increase in their salary. In addition to this, there was a beneficial profit-sharing plan available to staff. For example, if technical employees within the company introduced a money-saving idea, their bonus was closely related to the profit, or the additional profit, resulting from this initiative. It quite often occurred that some of the technical staff could get a bonus of several million RMB a year due to the high profit that was generated by the innovations that they had developed and that were adopted by the company.

A minor initiative introduced by management, as part of the on-going training programme available to all employees, was that management would give as a gift to the employees a number of books every year. The books were, of course, related to management, economics, or technical knowledge that was considered to be required by the employees for their job. The board of directors then encouraged employees to read the books, and then to write their views of the material they were given. This provided a reflective thinking focus on the texts that the staff were given, and allowed them to perform at a higher level by thinking critically of many of the daily tasks and issues that were faced by both themselves and of the organisation. The employees had to relate the material they read to the daily problems that they faced. The value of this initiative was demonstrated in the improved problem-solving skills of staff.

The company also provided training to the employees by allowing them to volunteer to transfer to other departments or organisations on a 'loan' basis to learn and to further develop their skills. If the employees demonstrated that their interest and capability was sufficient, CEC encouraged this development by further providing the employees with the opportunity to work in different environments. This demonstrated the flexibility of CEC in making the best use of the potential of their employees within the organisation.

A number of social activities were organised for all employees to allow them to team build with fellow employees within the company. This provided recreational activities to employees and various special interest clubs and family-related social activities were also encouraged.

To ensure the care of its migrant workers, the company assisted them by providing clean and safe accommodation. For those who did not live near the factory, further assistance was given by checking the safety of the accommodation for staff and their families. A family focus was demonstrated, which also assisted in staff retention within the organisation by giving help to those who had children in choosing appropriate schools.

Integral to the company is its recreational and facility focus, which can be demonstrated in the example of the provision of canteen facilities. These tended to be very crowded at meal times. One of the managers found that, due to the overcrowding at the staff canteen, many employees had to go to food sellers, located outside the factory, to purchase their meal. The manager then tried some of these places himself and found that the flavour of the food was lacking as compared to what was available in the staff canteen. As a result of this research, the manager made the recommendation that the staff canteen be increased in size to reduce or eliminate the need for staff to look elsewhere for their meal. Within three months the staff canteen was doubled in size and this allowed all employees to actually purchase their meal at a better quality and price than the food available outside the company gates.

A final key factor that contributed to the motivation of staff, as well as having the positive effect of reducing turnover of valued employees within the company, was the reputation of CEC. The company enjoyed a very high reputation compared to similar industries, and because of that, many of the employees felt proud to be working, and to be associated, with CEC. It was viewed as an employer of choice.

Other operational improvements

At the operational level, a 'Just in Time' (JIT) philosophy was adopted to ensure that goods and raw materials were not purchased until prior to their being needed. This reduced the inventory of stock being held by the organisation, thus saving space and possible interest payments as a result of paying for and holding material that was not being immediately used. The cost saving that resulted was used for further staff improvements.

Conclusion

With the changes in organisational structure and the hiring of appropriate management that fitted in with the culture and caring philosophy of the company, staff turnover was minimal and all employees worked in a stable and motivational environment. This approach further enhanced the reputation of the company as a family organisation and as an employer of choice. The opportunities to develop and be promoted within the company, with suitable training given to staff are important, as the company is sufficiently large to have a number of suitable career paths for employees who demonstrate potential.

The company's family focus extended to assisting employees to find safe and suitable accommodation, schooling for their children and ensuring that families remained together if possible. As the organisation becomes larger and more successful it will be interesting to see if many of the traits remain, or whether it will lose this ability in the battle to remain profitable in an increasingly competitive environment. The organisational commitment that exists in the company has so far resulted in the success of the business, as demonstrated by its growth. This commitment, coupled with the effective leadership style and staff engagement, should work towards ensuring the viability of the company over time.

References

Allen, N. and Meyer, J. (1990) 'The measurement and antecedents of affective continuance and normative commitment to the organisation', *Journal of Occupational Psychology*, **63**: 1–18.

Babcock-Roberson, M. and Strickland, O. (2010) 'The relationship between charismatic leadership, work engagement and organizational citizenship behaviours', *The Journal of Psychology*, **144**(3): 313–26.

De Lange, A., De Witte, H. and Notelaers, G. (2008) 'Should I stay or should I go? Examining longitudinal relations among job resources and work engagement for stayers and movers', *Work & Stress*, **22**(3): 201–23.

Howell, J. and Shamir, B. (2005) 'The role of followers in the charismatic leadership process: relationships and their consequences', *Academy of Management Review*, **30**(1): 96–112.

Hui, C., Lee, C. and Rousseau, D. (2004) 'Psychological contract and organizational citizenship behaviour in China: investigating generalizability and instrumentality', *Journal of Applied Psychology*, **89**(2): 311–21.

Landry, G., Panaccio, A. and Vandenberghe, C. (2010) 'Dimensionality and consequences of employee commitment to supervisors: a two-study examination', *The Journal of Psychology*, **144**(3): 286–312.

Organ, D. (1990) 'The motivational bases of organizational citizenship behaviour', cited in Hui, Lee and Rousseau (2004) 'Psychological contract and organizational citizenship behaviour in China: investigating generalizability and instrumentality', *Journal of Applied Psychology*, **89**(2): 311–21.

Yu, B. and C. Egri (2005) 'Human resource management practices and affective organisational commitment: a comparison of Chinese employees in a state-owned enterprise and a joint venture', *Asia-Pacific Journal of Human Resources*, **43**(3): 332–60.

Remuneration and retention in a privately-owned technology company

Introduction

As with many other organisations in China, Guangdong Waterproofing Technologies is having trouble attracting and retaining suitable staff. This company is using a number of attraction techniques based on remuneration and profit-sharing, along with assistance from the local government to attract young workers to the province. These younger workers, however, are not targeted specifically for this industry, and the company has to compete with other businesses that are experiencing similar problems in attracting and retaining staff in the area.

Remuneration is one tool that the organisation is using as a retention strategy. The remuneration techniques used are a form of gain-sharing to certain of the employees, in which a percentage of the profit is given to staff members who are at a certain management level in the company. Other employees do get a bonus, but this appears to be given without any strategy behind the process. Also, the gain-sharing could be viewed as inequitable, as all employees do not participate equally in this scheme. At this stage the company has not considered other methods to retain staff.

Literature review

Private enterprises have contributed significantly to China's recent economic growth and will continue to play a crucial role in its future development. However, Cheng et al. (2009) posited that certain factors hindered the development of Chinese private enterprises. For instance, more value has been attached to finance and marketing, rather than staff motivation and retention. More problems exist in their HR management systems, such as limited sources for recruiting new staff, a lack of sense of identity in employees due to family control of resources, no systematic performance management and compensation systems, and more reliance on physical and other extrinsic rewards than on intrinsic motivational factors.

Wang (2004) conducted a survey among private enterprises in Zhejiang Province, in the southeastern part of China and found that salary increases, physical rewards and promotion together account for 77.38 per cent of total motivation approaches in those companies surveyed, with the least attention being given to staff training, only 9.17 per cent.

However, a survey among knowledge-based employees in private enterprises presented a contrasting situation. Chen et al. (2005) found that intrinsic motivators were ranked much higher than extrinsic motivators among employees in the private companies investigated. This is explained as the aspiration for opportunities of self-realization, which is more possible in private enterprises due to their flexibility. Kyriacol (2010) also considered that selected incentives (including recognition) may also contribute to group motivation. Coinciding with the view of Chen et al. above, these motivators are more easily introduced in the private sector. In the Chinese context, however, it is possible that greater effort in acknowledging staff will be required for a private enterprise due to the lower commitment to remain in this type of organisation.

Li and Zhang (2005) found that the need level of employees in private enterprises tends to be lower than that found in state-owned enterprises. They explained it as less commitment and confidence of employees in the private enterprises. The reasons for this are not entirely clear but it is possible that in some areas of China, government employment is still viewed as preferable to private employment, despite the push to encourage private companies.

Sun (2008) studied the motivation of core employees in private enterprises from a psychological contract perspective and proposed that those companies involve core employees in the design of their own compensation package and also in other decision-making processes, linking their career plan to organisational growth and thus improving their employability. Li and Sun (2009) suggested that stock ownership by managers has a positive effect on organisational performance of these staff, while Wen (2009) proposed annuity as a cost-efficient approach for the private companies to motivate and retain their staff.

Another method that could be used is that of gain-sharing, a type of group incentive plan where any increase in profit could be shared equally among the group of managers (Milkovich and Newman, 2008). While this may motivate the management staff and also work to retain them within the organisation, unless it is expanded to all staff, retention of other employees would not necessarily occur. Clark et al. (2010) found that staff would compare their earnings, and if there was a great disparity between wages, salary or bonus, work effort would diminish. So although the incentives may result in higher motivation on the part of senior managers, motivation could easily diminish among other staff, with the strong possibility of them looking for other work in industries in which their efforts would be better rewarded.

It is possible that other methods could be introduced to encourage employees to remain. One possibility is the embeddedness approach. The concept of job embeddedness examines the links and fit of people and their jobs, and the ease in which these links can be broken (Mitchell et al. 2001). It examines the numerous factors that ensure people remain in their current jobs. Managers can strengthen the links by providing for their employees certain projects or tasks, or by increasing community involvement. Their research found that, even though employees may be satisfied with their current job and conditions, a low level of embeddedness may make them more open to certain factors which increase dissatisfaction. Thus the emphasis on job satisfaction and money may be limiting in its approach to ensure that employees remain in their job.

The organisation

Guangdong Waterproofing Technology was established in 2005. It is a high-tech enterprise located in a coastal city in Guangdong province in China. It was one of the hundreds of private enterprises which received special support from the local municipal government, to encourage businesses to set up operations in the province. The organisation currently has 50 employees, and its main product is waterproofing materials for use by industry. The main use of these materials is in the manufacturing of highways, tunnels and bridges, to provide protection against water damage.

It was founded under the leadership of scientific and technical staff located in the province, where it was acknowledged that there was a need for these materials to allow the expansion of much of the infrastructure in China. The company, specialising in geo-synthetic materials, owns a number of production lines, and produces a number of products for both government and industry.

With the development of the company, great efforts have been made to create an environment of science and technology, attracting a number of returned overseas university graduates among which one is a high-level waterproofing technology specialist, one holds a doctoral degree, and three hold Masters degrees. Permeation proof technology has gradually developed as the core technology of the company, and the business has grown into a comprehensive technology and production enterprise with its product range being expanded from original geo-synthetic materials to building waterproofing, permeation-proofing, construction reinforcement and ecological construction.

The business is mainly focused within China, supplying to a local market. There are hopes, however, that continued success will enable it to expand internationally into other markets. These opportunities are currently being explored, and there are to date a small number of international customers. Its products have been sold throughout the country, including Hong Kong and Macao, and widely used in many national major infrastructure projects such as railways, expressways, water conservation, subways, tunnels, landfills and land created by reclamation from the ocean.

The problems

The main problem facing the company was its high turnover of staff. This caused issues in production and continuity, and it added to the expenditure on training of the newly-recruited staff, causing excessive training costs to be incurred. As it is a high-technology organisation, the training of the new staff, although necessary, can also be quite expensive. These staff can also use the new skills that had been taught to them to negotiate a higher salary in other local companies, thus causing a continual training cost to the organisation.

The organisation does have an exit interview process for departing employees, to determine the reasons for departure. It was found through these interviews that the major reason for the high level of staff turnover was the level of compensation that was given to the staff. The employees, on departure, stated that the pay given to them was not up to their expectations as compared to other local companies. Another less significant reason for the staff turnover, but just as important, was the management style of the organisation. This problem in management style happened because of the lack of coordination between the different departments within the company. Because of this many of the employees refused to take responsibility for the quality of the product or for the slower production rate.

In addition to the payment issue, normally when a new recruit joins the organisation they have had a previous discussion about the payment level being given to that employee. The new entrant normally agrees to the payment schedule being given, but unfortunately as the employee stays with the company for a longer period of time, they normally request more money to be given to them, based on inflation and the increasing skills and experience that are accrued by the staff member. The major reason for this demand for additional payments is the younger age of the new recruits, and the fact that they may need the money for family reasons, to set up their family home. They generally consider that the payment given is not sufficient for them to support their family.

The issue of the whole salary package is, of course, another concern. One part is the fixed payment or the base pay. Another component of the salary package is the potential to profit share. This payment normally is just passed on to mid-level management, where they share part of the profit of the organisation to supplement their income. The problem is that all the managers have different priorities and projects to focus their energy on. Because of the nature of the industry some of the projects are relatively longer than other projects. Some of the projects may last for up to two years or longer. The problem is that the profit does not arise until after the project is finished, so the manager and other staff who share in the profit-sharing scheme may have to wait for up to two years or longer to receive their portion of the profits coming from the completion of the job. This time period between task completion and reward for the effort expended was considered as unsatisfactory by many of the staff.

Many of the employees, it was found, were not sufficiently patient to wait until the conclusion of the project. This problem is especially prevalent with fresh new university graduates. Although they say that they will stay with the company for the long-term, frequently many of them resign for other employment within a year. As mentioned earlier, they tend not to have the patience to wait until the conclusion of the project and to receive their fair share of the profits, even though the profit share could be quite substantial for a major project.

Although there was no firm resolution to this issue, the management did understand the problems facing the new employees. This is because of the pressure being placed on the company in the competitive environment and searching for staff in an increasingly tight skilled labour market, and also inflationary factors which cause the value of the employees' salaries to effectively decrease over a short period of time.

The solutions

Some of the suggestions proposed are:

1. Take on university students on a part-time basis and employ them under a traineeship scheme while they are continuing or completing their qualifications. This would enable them to commit to the organisation and receive payment while working, while also having money to assist with their studies. The guarantee of a job could also be used, further cementing the relationship and cooperation between the local universities and the company.

2. Provide assistance for existing employees to study on a part-time basis while working for the organisation. The caveat would be that the employees would have to remain with the organisation for a particular period of time in reimbursement for the fees that would be paid on their behalf. If the employees left their employment early, they would of course have to reimburse the organisation a pro-rata amount of money.

3. Pay the employees a percentage of the anticipated or expected profits of a long-term project while they are working on it. The problem with this, of course, is that it puts the company at risk if the profits do not materialise.

4. Form a number of social activities to engage the employees. This tends to make the organisation more family-focused and oriented, bringing in a form of employee embeddedness.

Training has already been provided to many of the employees within the organisation. This training tended to be not very expensive at the individual level. It focused on improving the skills of the employees, especially those employees who showed promise towards development and promotion within the organisation. The problem with the bond issue, in which employees would promise to work for a particular period of time and in return would have their fees paid for certain relevant courses, is that many people did not want to be tied to a particular organisation. They would be very reluctant to sign a contract which bonds them to the organisation for a number of years. Skilled people do not want to be limited by any form of contract that inhibits their mobility within the Chinese labour market.

There is a problem with paying a percentage of the profit to the employees, especially before full payment had been given to the company for their work. Guangdong Waterproofing Technologies is one of the growing number of small to medium enterprises in Guangdong Province. One of the most difficult situations that the small to medium enterprises face in smaller cities located in the province is the ability to raise finance. Sometimes it can be very difficult for them to raise sufficient funds to support this pre-profit-sharing initiative. This poses great risk to the organisation, as if they adopted such a proposal, they would be hoping that the projects would return a good profit to pay back any pre-bonus given to employees. The other issue is that they may have to borrow the money, thus incurring a debt and interest payments to a lending institution.

Although the social activity aspect had been investigated, the company had not fully implemented a social environment for staff. They are currently examining support for younger staff members, but no firm decision had been made as to the best way to implement family-friendly policies.

Another embeddedness aspect involves providing staff with interesting projects. Some form of intrinsic incentive could be tied to this project on its successful completion, thus raising the status of individual employees.

'Flow-back'

It was found that there is an interesting phenomenon with the company. This is the 'flow back' of employees to the organisation. The previous policy of the organisation was not to allow an employee to return once they had actually resigned from the company. However, recently there was an excellent employee who had left the company and then wished to return. This employee had made some money and wanted to form his own company, but this venture was unsuccessful. This employee was allowed to return to the organisation and is now one of the better workers. To date the company has rehired three employees who had previously left and then wished to return due to the better conditions within the organisation.

It must also be noted that the more mature workers, those in their thirties and forties, tended to have a stronger commitment to the company than the younger workers who had just graduated from university. These were the ones for whom career paths could be organised. Other options, of course, may be social activities being organised for workers at different levels within the company, looking at integrating the employees into a family environment.

Core employee plan

The company also considered introducing a core employee plan. The core employee is the head of each department within the company. There are now approximately 10 core employees. These employees tend to get better benefits the longer they stay with the company. Management has set certain production and sales targets for them, with the current sales turnover being around 60 to 70 million RMB a year. The anticipated sales target is expected to grow rapidly, with a greater demand for the products, to 200 million RMB a year over the next few years.

The profit margin of the company is 20 per cent, so the sales employees were told that if it was possible for them to maintain or increase their sales to this target, thus improving the profitability of the company, their bonus would increase. Conversely, if profits decreased, the bonus would obviously reduce. As a result of the bonus profit plan, it would become quite possible for individual employees to get up to 100,000 RMB per year in bonuses. This compares favourably with the target sales of the organisation of 200 million RMB, and it is obvious that the higher target sales will overall improve the company's standing.

As a result of this proposal, the board of directors agreed to take 10 per cent of the total profit to give to the employees as a bonus, but to be based solely on their performance. The target turnover for the core employees was estimated to be between 50 and 60 million RMB per person, and it would be quite possible for the sales employees to individually achieve sales of up to 100 million RMB per person per year. The overall sales target of the company was 200 million RMB per year. The profit margin to the organisation is approximately 20 per cent of turnover or return on spending, after all costs have been considered.

If the salespeople could manage to obtain this turnover per person of 100 million RMB, that equates to 20 million RMB profit to the organisation, coming from each individual salesperson. That, therefore, is equal to 2 million RMB, being 10 per cent of the 20 million RMB profit. This was a significant motivator to these core employees. To summarise, each core employee could then get (up to) approximately 200,000 RMB additional income per year, a substantial bonus.

Unfortunately, many of the employees were not sufficiently patient to wait for this end of year bonus. They considered that the bonus should be paid earlier. A number of the core employees, however, believed in this profit gain which would be given to them at the end of the year. This tended to be a motivator for many of the employees to stay within the company and not to look for employment elsewhere.

A problem, however, is that there are only so many core employees, with many more employees not being eligible for this gain-sharing arrangement. So the question of course is, what is the criteria for the core employees? The core employees are the heads of the different departments within the organisation, such as finance, marketing, sales and quality assurance, among other areas. Guangdong Waterproofing Technologies did find a barrier or problem in expanding the title of core employees to lower levels of employees within the company, as many of these are only manual workers. The company, at the moment, does not have sufficient confidence in many of the employees to give them the role or title of core employee. All of the core employees are familiar with the finances of the organisation, so they know the extent of profit that the company makes. Management of the organisation does not want all of the employees, including the front-line employees, knowing the extent of profit that the company makes. They maintain that this information should be confidential. Many of the lower-level employees do not have the level of commitment to the organisation that the core employees already have. There may, however, be reasons for this that relate to the allocation of these large bonuses and by not allowing employees to have some knowledge of the operations of the organisation, some uncertainty as to its viability may also contribute to the high staff turnover.

All employees of the organisation do, however, get a bonus, although they are not told that it is a profit sharing or gain-sharing plan. This bonus is part of the overall salary package of the employees. Their salary package is composed of two parts. The first part is the core salary, and the second part is their bonus or gain sharing aspect of the salary. This bonus is, of course, substantially smaller on a percentage base than the bonus given to the core employees of the organisation. It would not be possible to provide to all staff a similar incentive arrangement as the one given to the core staff members. There is also no consistency in the bonus given to employees as a result of this system.

Government assistance

It has proven difficult to attract potential employees to Guangdong Province. So to help new industry, a Technology Park has been set up as an incubator in which to 'nurture' new business in the area, and to provide employment as an attractor for young families to come to work in the city.

Some of the incentives provided have included assistance with housing, reduced taxes and assistance with migration. Other forms of assistance have included encouraging major universities to set up campuses in the province, and a greater provision of amenities, such as schools and hospitals.

A major problem, though, is retaining the younger graduates and workers in the area. The reason for the drift is that, although the province is near the coast and is in a very attractive area of China, young workers are persuaded by businesses in the larger cities (such as Guangzhou and Shanghai) to migrate there, even though the quality of life may not be as good.

Conclusion

This chapter has looked at the way in which a company is trying to tackle staff turnover through the use of remuneration tools. By using a gain-sharing bonus plan, it has succeeded in retaining the 'core employees' or senior management, but is having mixed success in keeping the other employees. The matter of pre-bonus is quite contentious, and it is doubtful that an organisation would pay a bonus on a project for which they have not yet been paid. If the business lost money as a result of the project, it would be impossible to claim that money back from the employees.

The financial support for training has merit, but staff are, understandably, reluctant to bond themselves to a company for a period of time. This bonding would limit their flexibility to move, should other better opportunities present themselves. An argument against this proposal is that the company should invest in training in any case, as it may be just as liable in recruiting staff who had been trained by other industries. Unfortunately, this perception remains among many companies in the country.

The government assistance that is provided to entice new employees to the area would have limited effect on the company, as it is more a general investment in the area rather than a focus on a specific organisation. It is really the role of the company to do its own searching for staff.

References

Chen Yunjuan, Zhang Xiaolin and Zhang Liangzhen, (2005) 'An empirical study on motivators to knowledge-based employees in private enterprises', *Journal of Hehai University (Social Sciences)*, 2: 25–8.

Cheng Lihua, Liang Pingfeng and Chen Jingjing (2009) 'On motivation management in private enterprises', *Productivity Research*, 8: 146–8.

Clark, A., Masclet, D. and Villeval, M. (2010) 'Effort and comparison income: experimental and survey evidence', *Industrial and Labor Relations Review*, **63**(3): 407–26.

Kyriacou, A. (2010) 'Intrinsic motivation and the logic of collective action', *The American Journal of Economics and Sociology*, **69**(2): 823–39.

Li Bin and Sun Yuejing, (2009) 'Relationship among stock ownership, restriction level and organizational performance – an empirical study on listed private companies', *China Soft Science*, **8**: 119–31.

Li Zhi and Zhang Hua (2005) 'A study on characteristics of needs and motivation of employees of high-level education in private enterprises', *Science Research Management*, **26**(6): 68–72.

Milkovich, G. and Newman, J. (2008) *Compensation.* (8th Ed.) Boston: McGraw-Hill Irwin.

Mitchell, T. R., Holtom, B. C., Lee, T. W., Sablynski, C. J. and Erez, M. (2001) 'Why people stay: using job embeddedness to predict voluntary turnover', *Academy of Management Journal*, **44**(6): 1102–21.

Sun Fanghua (2008) 'Core staff motivation in private enterprises – from the perspective of psychological contract', *Economic Forum*, **5**: 86–8.

Wang Xinwei (2004) 'Statistical analysis on motivation system in Zhejiang private enterprises', *Journal of Shaoxing University*, **24**(10): 71–4.

Wen Chunling (2009) 'An analysis of establishing annuity plan in private technology-based companies from the perspective of compensation motivation', *Productivity Research*, **24**: 204–6.

Organisational change at a multinational gas corporation in Shanghai

Introduction

The change from a controlled to a more open economy has been occurring at a relatively rapid pace in China. Many of the state-owned enterprises are either undergoing a privatisation process or are becoming joint venture operations with western multinational enterprises. This has had an impact on the organisational culture of both the management and the individual employees, and the pace of change, which has been incremental, has been met with some resistance.

The ability of employees to cope has been outstanding, but the ability of the foreign companies to adjust to changing conditions in a different environment also needs to be noted. This chapter deals with a major Chinese gas supplier and distributor, the challenges faced on both sides as a result of a takeover and the resultant necessary changes in the areas of safety and finance. Resistance to the change processes and the remedies used to overcome that change are noted.

Literature review

Technological advancement, changes in customer needs and the importance of creating value for customers have led, to a large extent, to organisational changes needing to be implemented in many companies (Mi and Huang, 2005). However, resistance is almost inevitable, especially when the organisational culture also needs to be changed.

One source of resistance is employees, who, sometimes having problems in receiving sufficient information, may feel a loss of established interest and be unable to adapt to changes (Lu, 2005; Li, 2007). Apart from individual employees, resistance to changes can also come from the organisational level, such as incompatible organisational structure, rules and regulations, as well as from within the existing culture of the management (Lu, 2005; Li, 2007).

Lewin (1951) developed an early model of change describing it as a three-stage process including unfreezing, changing and refreezing. In order to make changes easier, the organisation can try to reinforce the discontent of the employees about the existing conditions during the unfreezing process, show empathy towards employees while changing, and consolidate the achievements through intrinsic and extrinsic motivation in the refreezing stage (He, 2008). Similarly, Lu (2005) and Li (2007) both mentioned that proper motivational approaches played a vital role in helping to advance changes in an organisation.

To overcome the resistance encountered in the change process, it is necessary for the organisation to improve internal communication (Li, 2007) to ease employee tension caused by the change (Wang, 2008). This purpose can also be fulfilled by ensuring employee involvement during the change (Lu, 2005).

Besides this, leadership is of great importance in the changing process as Li (2007) proposed that the role of a change champion and a spiritual leader was irreplaceable. Both transformational and transactional leadership exert a positive effect on organisational changes. Which approach is more effective is contingent upon various situational factors (Mao and Long, 2008). What is more, experiential learning and recruiting fresh blood into the organisation can break employees' long-held views about the current situation and thereby will help to facilitate change (Wang, 2008).

Training is extremely necessary because it can help employees enhance their competency and therefore better adapt to change (Lu, 2005; Wang, 2008). Employee self-performance management helps to reduce the cost of changes both in financial and time terms (Zhang, 2008). The organisation can also offer gain-sharing schemes to overcome the resistance incurred by the loss of established interest (Wang, 2008).

During the change, the human resources department has many things to do to ensure smooth transitions in the above-mentioned functions (Ke and Pei, 2008). HR may be responsible for designing a new selection, evaluation, and compensation system to facilitate the changes. Besides, HR plays a large role in promoting changes in the existing corporate culture (Wang, 2007). According to Hu Hongliang et al. (2003), mid-level management also plays multiple roles in implementing changes in the organization, such as that of idea generator, communicator, counsellor and collaborator.

The organisation

MNC Gases (MNCG), a multinational corporation located in Shanghai, has a large presence in China and has seen the changes that occurred from the Chinese organisation being a fully state-owned enterprise to becoming a joint venture and there have been substantial changes in this evolution.

MNCG (China) initially started business in Shanghai in 1988, as a joint venture. Typically in those days when multinational corporations came into China to form joint ventures, they wanted to take over control of all employees. Many existing state employees went into the joint venture. However, employment was 'iron rice bowl' clad; the employees would not leave and could not be fired, as they were guaranteed jobs for life under the conditions that currently existed within China. Secondly, many of the state-owned enterprises were very old and traditional companies, and they had groups of employees who were quite old. There was no possibility of these employees being pressured into retirement to bring in a new cultural approach, with the younger or newer employees bringing in a fresh perspective.

Typically for MNCG, their policy was to go in with at least 50 per cent ownership of the joint venture, prefering to be a majority shareholder and have overall managerial control. This was found in the past to be an effective way, as far as MNCG was concerned, to allow it to introduce its policies, systems and processes and more importantly, its safety practices. Its global emphasis was on safety. This control was therefore as much from a profit perspective as well as a safety perspective. This was due to the nature of the product; gases are highly explosive so it is a potentially dangerous industry.

However, from about 1998 to 2002 the Chinese Government discouraged full ownership by an outside (China) firm. This acted as an inhibitor to MNCG introducing many of their management, safety and HR practices and procedures into the company in the first instance.

Areas of change/challenge

One of the most important challenges, supported by much of the literature, is to change people's mind-sets. It goes into many areas in terms of management practices. Safety and finance are two examples of this, and these were two areas of concern for MNCG. Taking it to the next step, one was to do with processes (the way of doing things) and the other to do with procedures (the steps that need to be taken).

The safety issue

Being an industry that is involved in the production and distribution of hazardous materials, safety was always a prime concern to MNCG. The state-owned enterprise, in the opinion of its new British partner, had some safety standards but the rules and enforcement of those rules was not of the standard expected. For example, under the rules of the state-owned enterprise, smoking was only allowed in certain designated areas. A first warning was given if an employee was caught smoking in a prohibited area. For the second instance, a serious warning was given, and for the third instance, the employee was dismissed. MNCG's new policy, however, was more direct. The first time an employee was caught smoking it resulted in an immediate dismissal for that person.

This change of mindset to a focus on safety required a break in the habits which had been acquired over many years of working in an state-owned environment, even though implementation of the new standards was straightforward. Employees were trained in the new safety requirements and advised of the implications of breaching these requirements. Notwithstanding this, habits do die hard and there was a case of a tanker driver who was dismissed for smoking taking his case to the local arbitration court over alleged wrongful dismissal.

The financial issues

The second issue was related to the financial aspects of the organisation, specifically relating to authorisation of expenditure. There appeared to be no knowledge of limits of expenditure, and managers were effectively given an open policy on their delegation, with no or minimal monitoring. The problem that existed was how to gain acceptance from people for the kind of changes that needed to be made on these policy matters, as the organisation under its new owners needed to make a profit and it could be seen that the lack of delegated authority would be an inhibiting factor in the process. This aspect can then be broken into two components of the problem. The first is standards and the second is processes.

Authorisation policy

Multinational corporations have a stringent compliance on authorisation of expenditure. Being a listed company in both London and New York, MNCG and many other companies have very stringent compliance requirements on both financial and legal reporting. Leadership in these aspects of management sets both example in practice and in the pace of change occurring. The management have to set the example as they have a high profile among employees. Any transgression on their part results in a loss of faith on the part of the employee. Flexibility can be allowed but certain regulations are non-negotiable.

The Chinese way of doing things tends to be too flexible, and it is well known among expatriate management that the Chinese people do not like regulations and will not follow them. They also do not like monitoring or follow-up. The core issue behind this is to do with leadership setting the examples and the pace. Leaders have a very high profile, and therefore in a society like China, whatever leaders do, the rest tend to follow.

The Chinese way of doing things is very much a 'follow-ship'. The concept of empowerment, especially in the early days, was alien in China. This brings into the equation the notion of Guanxi, which is based on a Confucianist ideal and includes things such as respect for elders, seniority and authority.

The initial problem to resolve, then, is how to change the mindset of both management and employees. This is difficult when senior people, at the social level, need to understand, accept and live by the rules in the Chinese context, while living and working in China. However, it can still be changed if a better approach can be demonstrated to the employees. This is done through the process of communication and training. In the communication sessions, the trainer needs to show employees the benefits of the change process. To provide this training, MNCG developed a corporate culture training programme called ACTS: A is for accountability, C is for collaboration, T is for transparency and S is for stretch.

Accountability was a fairly alien concept in Chinese society. Employees tended to mix accountability with responsibility. But accountability has a further step, and that is the question of 'answerability'. In other words, you answer for whatever you do. It is not just the responsibility. In China, responsibility is considered to be a task. You are assigned a task and that is it. Whether you do it well, badly, or do not even complete it, you are not answerable for it.

So at MNCG, the way that the Chinese employee defined a given term first needed to be examined. The Chinese perspective was studied and understood from this unique point of view. What were the critical differences and similarities of the same term taken in a multinational context? Ability is one, but substantial emphasis is also placed on collaboration. With collaboration, the organisation is not just talking about a corporate image. They need to go one step beyond that. When managers talk about collaboration, they talk about all needing a common objective to allow this collaboration. Different departments will have different objectives, but at an industry level and at a country level, collaboration leads to the achievement of a common objective.

The objective

One example of achieving a common objective is that of finance. The finance department loves to collect money, but salespeople love to make their customers happy, and find it hard to press them for payment. Finance then finds it unacceptable that payment is delayed. How is this problem resolved so that the common objective of making money can be achieved?

The answer is to resolve it with common bonding, a common aim or shared objective. If a customer does not pay, does the organisation really need or want this customer? How far will an organisation let a customer take this liberty of not paying debt owed to the company? Where does it stop? Must there be endless debt? By asking these questions, staff in both finance and sales realise that there is a common bond. That common bond or goal is what the organisation called its strategic objective.

This, then, brings up the issue of transparency. The organisation should not necessarily tell the whole world about changes that are going on, but should concentrate on the parties that are directly affected internally and externally. Management need to know who to give information to and who to share information with. There needs to be a balance between confidentiality and the need to share valuable information with employees. This is the value of transparency, where an employee should be willing to go beyond what they need to do and be given the information to do this.

For example, if management gives its employees a Key Performance Indicator (KPI) of 100, a good employee should aim to meet a personal objective at a higher level, say 106. They are then giving the manager 6 per cent above what is being asked. If they over extend their KPI, for example to 140, that can be very unrealistic and many employees will fail if they try to set unrealistic goals.

As discussed earlier, the major area that needed to be emphasised by MNCG was that of safety. This needed to be broken up into behaviour-based versus process-based aspects. From this perspective, it was more important to confine it to process.

The financial process, however, is essential if the organisation is to grow and thrive. When a multinational enterprise enters into a joint venture, it does what is called a due diligence test. Part of the due diligence process is looking at various items within the organisation, looking at the various setbacks the organisation may have suffered, and as a result, putting a number of improvements into place.

A practical setback that MNCG suffered was the limits on authority placed on management in China. The philosophy is that whatever the senior man says, goes. So in a factory environment, whatever the factory manager says, goes. There appeared to be no understanding of the limit of authority for each and every level within the organisation and this had to be introduced at the conceptual level in terms of both breadth and depth. It was necessary to look at the area that a particular person was responsible for, asking questions such as how much can a cheque be signed for, how much can you approve capital expenditure for, and what is the authority to approve daily expenses. This is commonly known as delegated authority.

It was then necessary to explain to the employees and management why this limit of authority was necessary. As mentioned previously, the Chinese employees did not have any understanding of the concept. For them, the limit of authority of the local authority, in the past, may have been the emperor of the country. At the county level, it may have been the county magistrate. However, within an organisation, there could be many different levels of authority. The difficulty was educating all employees about the different levels of responsibility and authority, and a deeper problem was to ensure that people auditing at those levels of authority were aware of this. It was not only necessary to talk about the 'what' and the 'how', but also to talk about the 'why'. Knowing the 'what' is the knowledge, knowing the 'how' is the application, but knowing the 'why' is the real understanding. So the problem was explaining to them why a delegation of authority or a limit of authority was actioned in the way it was.

All this was explained to them in these simple terms. There are certain areas in which the things cannot be questioned, such as the laws and regulations of the country. One never questions, for example, stopping at a red traffic light. The simple answer is that it is a regulation. Similarly, one never asks why 1 foot equals 12 inches. The reason is that it is a standard. In standards and regulations, there is no why, there is only acceptance. However, standards and regulations may be adjusted where prevailing conditions necessitate it. In areas such as health and safety and financial delegation, questions may be raised by people working within the organisation if they are not used to the rules and regulations that apply. Employees must realise that when a standard is changed, there may occasionally be unexpected results. Furthermore, if standards are dropped and overridden, the result may be increased wastage, causing the unit cost to go up. The organisation must decide if they could accept this. This is how the company conceptually changed the way the employees think.

When taking over or engaging in a joint venture, the use of senior management staff within the organisation is key. If the senior people within the organisation do not necessarily believe that what they are doing is necessary or beneficial, it is very difficult to implement any changes in policy, practice, rules and regulations or procedures. As a result, it is very important that people at this supervisory level, and people at the management level are aware of, and convinced by, the value of the change process. They need to have a strong commitment, and the new owners of the joint venture need to ensure that this commitment is followed through to result in exemplary conduct of managers and employees.

The next issue that the owners of the joint venture needed to look at was to identify who the employees and management identified as their champions within the organisation. They needed to be aware of resistant camps within the company, pin-pointing those people who were likely to resist the necessary changes. Once champions within an organisation have been identified, they are the best people to use as spokespersons to engage in the change process. For those who were resistant to the change process at MNCG, a number of discussion sessions were held with the champions to allow them to understand the reasons for the change. In this process a soft approach was desirable, to convince employees of the benefits of the change.

If all else failed, and the employees still refused to accept the change, a parting strategy could be employed. Of course, the severity of the resistance and the areas to which it relates needed to be examined. For a safety issue, there will not be any compromise; policy must stand, and the imperative of this policy needs to be communicated to all employees. The communications process is an extremely important part of the change.

In terms of leadership and authority, the various rules needed to cascade down from head office level into the smaller business units. The way that MNCG was structured in China was by line of business. Before 2000, it used to be by geographical region. China was carved into three regions, north-east, east and south. From 2000 onwards, however, it was divided by the line of business and further organised by product line. When MNCG implemented the new authorisation policy, it was common across all business units. Supporting functions like human resources, finance, quality assurance and others were common across all business units and were organised as shared services. Corporate functions, therefore, cut across the product line.

In any kind of change, there will be people who are adversely affected, and may then go against the change. There are people who are neutral, who are not positively or negatively affected by the changes. There will, however, be a small number of people who are positively affected. Their jobs may be made easier, or may be expanded. In other words, their authority may have been enhanced or diminished. Different people will be impacted differently as a result of these changes and resistance or acceptance will vary.

Those resistant to change can be broken into three categories. First, there are people who are very uncertain of the changes and do not know how to implement them. Second are people who are adversely affected and have the perception that their authority has been eroded. It is quite possible that these employees have jobs that have actually grown smaller. In the Chinese context, they could be seen as losing face and consider that they have effectively been demoted. Third are people who may resist the change process because they do not have the skills to actually cope with changes.

At MNCG the main area of resistance tended to come predominantly from those whose authority was not clearly stated in the past. This was because, theoretically, they had unlimited authority. Their delegated authority had not been clearly stated by the previous management. Similarly, it was found by a number of managers on their entry into the Chinese market, that the Chinese had a tendency to say, 'You did not say that I could not do it, so therefore I did it'. To re-phrase, the Chinese workers considered that if you did not state a limit, they could do anything without limit. Therefore, when an authorisation or delegation policy was introduced into the organisation, it was viewed by many as a restrictive covenant. It meant to them that they could only take action up to a certain stage. Beyond that they were forbidden to take any further action. As an example, looking at the area of financial delegation, certain employees may have been given the authority to sign cheques up to an amount of $1000. If they were requested to sign for a figure of, for example, $1020, they were not allowed to do so. It was explained to them that this was what the authorisation policy included. This was also what led to resistance in many quarters of the organisation, where people may have actually had unlimited authority or perceived that ultimate authority in the past. Now, however, a strict delegation was to be applied to the employees.

This then, was the problem that MNCG had to understand and modify. Because the delegation was applied to many people in the company, these managers and other employees thought that it was an erosion of their authority and therefore considered that they had lost face as a result of this policy.

This whole issue points to a cultural problem of the Chinese people. To understand it, expatriate managers need to understand and study how the problem evolved. The old management structure of the organisation did not get the Chinese employees to question the authority of the manager. In fact, they were definitely told not to question it. However, under the re-organisation, employees were advised that if they noticed that their manager was signing something that was contrary to the policy, this error or breach should be pointed out to the senior management.

Employees, who were auditing management expenditure, were given two options. They were advised in the first instance, to go back to the manager who signed it and bring the matter to his or her attention, raising the issue that they may not be aware of their delegated authority. The other option was to raise the issue with their manager. If they were an accountant, they would raise it with the accounting manager. They were advised that the best approach would be to mention to their manager that they consider that the manager may have made a mistake, in that he had signed an authority beyond his delegated expenditure. It was then the responsibility of the accounting manager to handle the issue.

Effectively, the expatriate managers were advising the finance department to check on what other managers and staff were doing. The reason for this is that the finance department was viewed as the last line of defence. If an over-expenditure passes through finance, it is already too late and costs the company money.

The initial training in the new regulations, therefore, was focused on the finance staff. It was found and acknowledged that in the initial period of training and acceptance of the new policy, there were a number of mistakes that would be made. Employees were either not too sure of the policy or were not familiar with its application. Because MNCG management expected a number of errors to be made, the situation was monitored very carefully. Corporate finance employees were advised to go to the supervisory and management level, and examine the documents. Effectively this was a snap audit. It was emphasised to employees that it was not a formal audit but was used to pick up small erroneous authorisations. This snap audit was done over a six-month period. The first three months involved the review of any errors. The second three-month period was to determine if there were any improvements. If it was found that there had been improvements made in the second three months, it would then be subject to a formal audit.

It must be admitted that there were mistakes made. People may have forgotten or misinterpreted the policy, or there were other reasons for these mistakes being made. However, over a given period of time, each finance meeting pointed out any discrepancies that were made. The intention was not to highlight these mistakes, but to let the employees share and learn from what each area had done. It was effectively a self-improvement exercise.

Conclusion

Many multinational enterprises have managers who are expatriates. It is important that these managers understand and know the local way of doing things. However, it must be acknowledged that foreign managers do face a number of difficulties. The manager must understand how much he or she can tolerate and how much cannot be tolerated, what must be done and done now and what can be done later. In other words, the manager will need an adjustment period.

There are exceptions, however. For example, in the issue of safety within MNCG and other multinational organisations, there was no room for compromise. When people's lives are at stake, there is no margin for error. With regard to the financial changes impacting on delegated authority, there was some leniency given to the initial implementation of the changes introduced to the organisation.

For these processes, an adjustment period should be given for the process-based change. Foreign managers need to be aware that a fine balance is required when implementing the changes. They need to understand what areas can be changed rapidly and what areas need caution in the change process, as well as the changing of existing mind-sets within the company. This brings an acknowledgement of the existing culture and a realisation that the locally-based culture needs to be taken into consideration.

References

He Xiaoli (2008) 'The effective motivational mechanism in organizational changes', *Management and Administration*, 3: 54–5.

Hu Hongliang, Chen Xudong and Xu Xiaodong (2003) 'A study on the role of mid-level management in organizational changes', *Management Modernization*, 1: 15–18.

Ke Jian and Pei Liangliang (2008) 'Human resource management approaches in organizational changes', *Human Resource Development of China*, 6: 10–13.

Lewin, K. (1951) *Field Theory and Social Science: Selected Theoretical Papers.* Harper and Row: New York.

Li Zuozhan (2007) 'Overcoming resistance in different organizational change patterns', *Modern Management Science*, 6: 45–6.

Lu Hong (2005) 'Reducing the resistance from employees in organizational changes', *Human Resource Development of China*, 2: 51–4.

Mao Minxin and Long Lirong (2008) 'An empirical study on relationship between leadership style and organizational change of service industry', *Industrial Engineering and Management*, 3: 73–84.

Mi Xuming and Huang Liming (2005) 'A study on affecting factors in the organizational changes', *Contemporary Economic Management*, 27(1): 43–5.

Wang Bingcheng (2008) 'Managing employee behavior in the context of organizational changes', *Human Resource Development of China*, 6: 20–2.

Wang Ruojun (2007) 'The supportive function of human resource management in organizational changes', *Human Resource Development*, 6: 18–20.

Zhang Yongsheng (2008) 'Employee self-performance management's driving effect on organizational changes', *Human Resource Development of China*, 6: 17–19.

15

Compensation strategies as a motivational and retention tool

Doug Davies, Liang Wei and Zhang Xinyan

Introduction

This chapter looks at the issue of compensation in a private company in China, coupled with the expansion of the business from a domestic operation to an international focus with mixed success. Commencing with an inequitable and illogical salary and bonus system, the organisation moved from a ranking system of evaluation to a points-factor system, and followed this with a stock option plan to improve retention and motivation, which resulted in creating more problems than it resolved. A form of gain-sharing was then introduced in its place, with better results. The case study also examines the evolving form of the company from a domestic to an international supplier and the mixed success in the subsequent restructure, with different incentive schemes in operation.

Literature review

Compensation consists of all forms of remuneration and associated benefits that are given to employees as part of their relationship with the employer (Milkovich and Newman, 2008). However, different employees are entitled to differing levels of pay depending on the role that is played within a company. Many employees may view their salary as inequitable compared to the effort that they put in, and this may be a de-motivator for these staff members (Henderson, 2006). To reduce the feeling of inequity and to improve motivation among employees, a performance based system can be used as well as other different systems, such as bonuses, piece-rates, stock options and profit-sharing to reward workers (Pouliakas and Theodossiou, 2009). However, there is little evidence to say for sure whether these plans have any effect at all on employee motivation and organizational outcomes (Kraizberg et al., 2002).

This does not stop a company, however, from using these plans to improve staff motivation, increase work performance and reduce turnover of employees. These different reward systems may all be available as a tool to the manager. Stock options are a choice for management personnel but there are potential problems that can result from the use of this strategy (Yermack, 1997), as highlighted in this case study. Gain-sharing is another incentive as such plans can work to gain the cooperation of employees in an organisation, and can be compatible with building the trust of staff (Chenhall and Langfield-Smith, 2003).

The organisation

The company is a private organisation located near Shanghai. It commenced operations in 1989 as a very small manufacturing and mechanical operations company. In the first few years of its operations it did not grow very much due to very few orders and a small market base. After three years, however, a decision was made to expand into car components and accessories manufacturing due to the increased number of vehicles coming into private use. Before 2000, the market of the organisation was predominantly domestic. After 2000, however, the decision was made to transfer the focus to an international context, by looking at potential buyers of their product in other countries, with the main focus of the marketing on North America.

Before 2002 the annual revenue of the company was approximately 60 million RMB a year. The management considered that further expansion, both domestically and internationally, would result in a greater profit due to the lower salaries of the employees and the greater efficiency of the company.

The problem

The major difficulty in the organisation was the compensation system. There was no transparency existing in the compensation that was paid to employees and how it was determined. The payment to staff was at a very low base rate. Even payment made to senior managers was extremely low, between 1000 RMB and 2000 RMB per month. However, the base pay was only about one quarter of the total income paid to the employees. The other component of the income was from the bonus that was paid at the discretion of the manager. The bonus was, to some extent, based on the performance of the employee, but to an equally large extent, it was based on the manager's view of the personality of the employee and how they associated with the management of the company. The manager had his own evaluation on performance, not based on any firm or set criteria, and this bonus was, therefore, paid at his whim. Effectively the payment system was inequitable as it was strongly based on the personalities within the company. In line with this, it was also based on the profit that the company had made in a particular time period.

This inequitable distribution of bonuses led to employees leaving at the end of each year, after they had been given their yearly bonus. Although the manager did not disclose the amount of bonus paid to each employee, it was quite common for the employees to actually compare their annual bonus with each other. If a substantial amount of inequity was found in the bonus given to staff, there was strong dissatisfaction. As a result of this, many employees considered the bonus paid was unfair, and resigned from the company.

So the problem was to maintain a certain transparency in the salary system, but also to use it as a motivator of staff. To try to reduce the high level of resignations occurring, and to improve the motivation of staff within the organisation, a private consulting company was brought in to look at the remuneration system. Their role was to change the compensation system and make it into a motivator and retainer of staff. The two issues that had to be considered were external equity and the other job opportunities that were available to employees if they considered that their pay was unfair. It was quite common for competitors to poach many of the staff from other companies in the region by offering a better and fairer remuneration system. As the industry was fast-growing, there were many competitors looking for suitable skilled and trained staff. Due to the shortage of these skilled staff, it was quite easy for many of the employees to find alternative employment with these other companies. If an employee was not satisfied with the bonus, they simply left and found another job. So the overriding issue was the market competitiveness of the compensation system.

Regarding employee benefits, the company did not provide even the most basic benefits system. Although the basic social welfare system that was legislated by the government was supposed to be implemented, the company did not support it. Generally it was considered mandatory to provide the employees with this sense of security and safety, but this obligation was lacking within the company.

It was also suggested by the consultants to the company that they build accommodation for their employees who came from other provinces or areas in China. The company did this. Prior to this the employees had to pay for their own accommodation and, considering the low wage that they received, many of them were living in hardship and only had basic rooms in dormitories as the salary was too low to allow them to move to better and safer rooms. The company was also made to establish a canteen for its staff, to provide at least basic meals to the employees.

The managers did not live in the dormitories. They were provided a subsidy by the company to manage their own apartment within the vicinity. Although this subsidy did not cover all of the rent costs, it did cover a substantial part of it. The only other benefits that they received was their end of year bonus. No other additional benefits were given to them. All managers at the same level received the same salary. Due to the intervention of the consultant, the line management structure was redrawn, to recognise the different levels of difficulty and expertise required for each position. A number of different lines, for example, the management line, the technical line, the professional line and the administrative line, were all then structured so as to recognise the different skill levels and work levels that occurred within those specific areas. Salary was adjusted accordingly. Salary levels were also varied to demonstrate the importance of certain of the functions of management within the company. For example, the marketing manager was considered to be more valuable than the manufacturing manager due to the difficulties in selling the products in a competitive environment.

This problem of the different pay levels of management was solved based on an examination of the payments made to staff in other organisations who were working at an equivalent level. A salary survey was done in the market to determine the salary levels paid to these different management levels. This revealed that many equivalent organisations paid less to the manufacturing manager than to the marketing manager. The salaries were then brought up to an equivalent level to external competition, making it less likely that employees would leave to work for a company that paid more, as salary levels were changed so as to be based on the market average.

A job evaluation was also done on all positions throughout the company to establish the importance and contribution of the differing departments. The initial job evaluation system was not complex. It was based on subjective criteria and was simply a basic ranking system which looked at the importance of the different roles undertaken by each staff member. It was examined again after a twelve-month period, when it was found that there were many problems existing in this current system. A new and improved system was examined for implementation at a later date. However, it was realised by employees that the company was at least trying to introduce a fairer system of compensation to eliminate many of the inequities that existed. The system was explained to all staff and the role of the manager of being the only person to decide on the allocation of bonuses was diluted to some extent. The system was administratively sound.

In 2004 more improvements were made to the system to ensure that equity considerations were further enhanced. The system of bonus allocation was implemented in a more systematic manner. This also relieved much of the pressure from the senior management in deciding who was to be paid what amount as a bonus.

Continuing changes

A number of incremental improvements have been made to the remuneration system over the past few years to further improve internal, external and individual equity considerations. The system has also been made more open so that all employees can understand how their salary is calculated and how their bonus is allocated. In 2004, a points factor system was introduced to evaluate all positions with the company. As this is a modification of the system that was brought in earlier, only a partial adjustment of the pay rates was required due to the general acceptance of the rates introduced as part of the initial restructure.

Organisational changes and the compensation problems

Coupled with the restructure of the compensation system, a restructure of the internal organisation was also carried out. Essentially, the relationship between the different departments was modified to accommodate the internal supply and customer relationships that were growing. This better integration of the differing departments made the company more competitive as compared with other manufacturers.

Human Resources Management in China

Also in 2004, because of the rapid rate of growth of the company, coupled with strong development of its financial strength (growing from 60 million RMB annually, to approximately 600 million RMB annually), the company had to recruit additional managers for a number of departments to assist in the manufacturing of the various components and overall management tasks.

Unfortunately, due to the introduction of a number of senior managers within the company, the existing managers were effectively downgraded, although they did not suffer a loss of pay. What actually happened, however, was that they lost some of their standing within the company. This had a major impact on their morale.

Although the original managers were effectively downgraded, it was not possible to lower their original salary to better reflect their changed roles. This was due to their contractual arrangements with the organisation. As a result of this, the total salary costs of the company increased. Due, however, to the rapid growth and increasing revenue of the company, they could afford this additional cost, although it was not a preferred position.

In 2006, the growth rate of the company slowed dramatically due to economic conditions at the time. Prior to this drop in revenue in 2006, a more aggressive marketing strategy was adopted to allow them to expand faster into the American market. Before 2004, they had actually entered the American market but through a middleman. In 2004, however, they decided to directly enter into the market without going through these various agents. They then negotiated a contract with one of the local American companies. This allowed them to do business with them, directly. It was actually a forward integration through the replacement of the representatives. Unfortunately this strategy was not successful. It ended up costing the organisation a substantial sum of money, as the local American companies had very strict requirements regarding quality and standard of goods. Substantial sums of money had to be spent to meet these requirements. This resulted in a large increase in costs to the company.

After that, management decided to expand their market scope by producing a greater variety of goods. This was due to the expenditures they had put in place retooling part of the organisation, and they decided that, as the money had already been invested in the new plant and equipment, the capacity was available to expand into other areas. Unfortunately, that project failed to ring in the expected orders, with no subsequent increase in revenue. Effectively, there was insufficient return on their investment.

180

Stock option plan

As well as substantially expanding the business, a stock options scheme for employees was designed in 2004 and implemented in 2005. The rationale behind this was to motivate employees, increasing their competitive nature through part ownership of the company, and to further assist in the expansion that was taking place. The first stock option deal covered approximately 20 of the managers. The beneficiaries of the stock option tended to be the newly recruited managers. However, a small number of the existing managers also were offered the stock options. The reason that the newer managers were offered the stock options in preference to many of the older managers was to encourage the new managers to participate more aggressively in the new marketing and manufacturing strategies. It was expected that as a result of this increased aggressiveness in marketing, sales would increase.

Although the stock options were beneficial in some respects to increased motivation of the managers, there was a downside to this. As a result of the over-expansion, the new managers had become wealthy because of the appreciation of the stocks, and they gained a greater amount of power in how the company was run, as they owned a percentage of the company as a result of their shares. The CEO, therefore, lost a substantial amount of power in the daily running of the company.

The benefits and problems of the stock option plan

All of the employees became very motivated as they all wished to have a share in the stock option plan that was being offered to them. At the organisational level, market share was expanding. However, profitability was decreasing due to the over-expansion of the organisation. Although the market share had increased, the profit margin per manufactured item was decreasing.

There were also a number of disadvantages within the stock option arrangement that were becoming evident. Although employees received a large sum of money through the stock option plan, some at the management level considered leaving the company in 2007. One reason for this was that, due to the reduced profit margin, pressure was increasing on staff to perform at a higher level. This made working for the company less attractive. As they had already received a large number of shares through the stock option process, the opportunity was there to sell their shares. This money that they had gained through the stock option process gave them the finances to commence their own operations in opposition to the original company.

That aside, in 2007 a smaller stock option plan was introduced, which was considered to be supplementary to the original plan. More shares were attributed to the two vice-presidents of the company who were the two most important people next to the CEO. This share plan was given to these people only in order to retain their services within the company. The decision was then made to extend it to key personnel within the company in order to retain their services and loyalty.

In 2008 and 2009, a third option was proposed. This was due to the decision by the two vice presidents to resign. Additionally, due to the departure or potential departure of many other key employees, the decision was made to close the stock option plan, and to introduce a profit-sharing plan within the company. This was along the lines of a gain-sharing plan.

Further organisational changes

Due to the expansion of the organisation, a number of sub companies were formed. The recommendation was made that all of the sub companies were to be built into the profit centre. For employees working in the centre of the organisation they would then participate in gain sharing, rather than the previous stock option plan. In 2009, a further reorganisation of the company was proposed. The parent company was reorganised into a profit centre based company. There were five profit centres that contributed to this central parent base. The first profit centre was the organisational and equipment manufacturing arm. The second was the import–export arm of the company. The third profit centre was the manufacturing arm of the organisation. The fourth centre was the international marketing department. The fifth centre was the domestic marketing department.

Prior to this, the emphasis was placed on the parent company with stock options. Now, however, the organisation has several profit centres. Nevertheless, due to the autonomy given to the profit centres, some of them will still use stock option plans for motivational purposes. This autonomy was given solely to the import-export profit centre. For the other companies, gain sharing was still being used as the preferred motivator.

Conclusion

This chapter examined the compensation strategies used by an organisation from a start-up company to a more developed business over a number of years. The initial and inequitable compensation system used was replaced on the suggestion of a consulting company by a more scientific method of remuneration, using a points-factor method of analysis coupled with an appropriate salary survey.

However, staff retention and motivation was still a matter of concern, which resulted in a stock option plan being introduced. This system ended up working against the company, with many senior staff selling their shares and going into competition against the original company. In its place a gain-sharing plan was implemented with better results.

References

Chenhall, R. and Langfield-Smith, K. (2003) 'Performance measurement and reward systems, trust, and strategic change', *Journal of Management Accounting Research*, **15**(1): 117–43.

Henderson, R. (2006) *Compensation Management in a Knowledge-Based World*. Englewood Cliffs, N.J.: Pearson.

Kraizberg, E., Tziner, A. and Weisberg, J. (2002) 'Employee stock options: are they indeed superior to other incentive compensation schemes?', *Journal of Business and Psychology*, **16**(3): 383–90.

Milkovich, G. and Newman, J. (2009) *Compensation* (9th edn). Boston: McGraw-Hill Irwin.

Pouliakas, K and Theodossiou, I. (2009) 'Confronting objections to performance pay: the impact of individual and gain-sharing incentives on job satisfaction', *Scottish Journal of Political Economy*, **56**(5): 662–84.

Yermack, D. (1997) 'Good timing: CEO stock option awards and company news announcement', *The Journal of Finance*, **52**(2): 449–76.

16

Performance management at International Air Transport

Introduction

This chapter examines staff motivation and its relationship to performance and compensation factors in a competition-intensive air freight transport industry. Poor customer service and the need to improve company image led to the integration of a number of human resource, marketing and management factors to resolve the problems in the company. Motivation was the major concern, a lack of which was leading to reports of poor customer service.

The introduction of a performance management system that was related to customer service and remuneration resulted in a reduction in customer complaints, higher staff morale and a better bonus and remuneration system for staff. This in turn resulted in an increase in business, compared to other freight transport companies in the area, due to the value-added attitude of the performance-managed employees.

Literature review

Motivation has always been a hot issue among Chinese researchers into business. In China, a large proportion of employees still tend to be motivated by money, and therefore direct financial compensation plays a large role in employee job satisfaction (Qiu Weinian, 2007). Consequently, compensation issues have continuously received wide attention as a major motivator of staff. Moreover, due to the significant influence of employee job satisfaction and organisational commitment on their turnover intentions (Ye Rensun et al., 2005), the study and application of compensation management practices in organisations is of great importance in assisting companies to retain their key employees.

Wu et al. (2006) conducted a survey among more than 800 employees in 10 hotels in Guangzhou (southern China) and found that equity in compensation management had a significant role in boosting an employee's sense of identity and was definitely a motivational factor in the organisation. This is similar to what Zheng and Lu (2008) found in their study, in which personal realisation and social status was also considered to be positively correlated with employee pay satisfaction in addition to organisation equity. On the other hand, equal payment to all staff, regardless of an employee's individual contribution or performance, is the main cause of a sense of inequity among the workers and, therefore, this can be a serious demotivator in the organisation (Li and Chen, 2008).

In 1983, Hochschild first put forward the concept of 'emotional labour', pointing out that in service industries, employees sell, not only the product and service, but also their attitudes, to the customers. Among other things, these include friendliness, smiles and a caring attitude. Thus, in order to motivate employees engaged in the emotional labour industry, companies have to build an equitable work atmosphere, through which they can help their employees maintain a light mood during the service-delivering process and thereby ensure that service quality is maintained (Zhang et al., 2007). Companies can also improve their internal equity in compensation management through a properly conducted job evaluation process and establishing among employees the concept of valid input (i.e. employees' inputs that could add to the company value) and total compensation (including financial compensation and training, promotional opportunities through a recognised career path, and other benefits) (Shao and Xu, 2004).

In addition, employee pay satisfaction should not be considered as a single-structure, but it can be further divided into four dimensions. These dimensions are pay structure satisfaction, pay level satisfaction, pay system satisfaction and benefit satisfaction. Managers have to be aware of the different dimensions contained in employee pay satisfaction before they can fully understand employee motivation and satisfaction (Wang Wei, 2004). Similarly, Liu and Jiang (2008) considered the employees' compensation equity structure as a four-dimension model as well, including distribution equity, leader evaluation equity, procedural equity and information access equity, of which the equity of leader evaluation had a significant predictive effect on employee performance, while the procedural equity, leader evaluation and information access had a significant predictive effect on employee commitment to the organisation.

This is a confirmation of the importance of the role of leaders or superiors in an organisation in the Chinese cultural context.

The organisation

International Air Transport (IAT) is involved in the express industry for air cargo transportation. IAT was formed in 1973 in the United States of America. It examined the growing Chinese market and commenced its operations there in 1984. Its Chinese operations now employ in excess of 6,000 staff. Services offered to customers of IAT in China include package delivery to any destination in the world and package delivery to customers in China for their import business.

The industry is mainly involved in logistics so many vehicles are required to maintain operations and to ensure quick and expeditious delivery for its customers. This includes a large and reliable fleet of aeroplanes and panel vans, as well as a highly efficient courier service, where the packages, once they have arrived by air, can be collected and delivered to the customers as efficiently as possible. The head office of the Chinese operation of IAT is located in Beijing, but the company is split up into three regional forces covering eastern, southern and northern China. There are three managing directors responsible for these operations, one being located in each of these regions.

The problem

The major problem facing IAT was motivation of their staff, specifically related to compensation issues. How to motivate the front-line employees was a major concern to management of the organisation. Without the motivation of staff it was very difficult to give the high quality of customer service that managers promised to their customers. Logistics is a service quality industry, and it is very important for the company to guarantee that the customer is well supported and has no problems. This ensures repeat business, which is an important issue due to the competitive nature of the industry.

For many years IAT has provided good customer service and excellent customer service quality and they hope that each of the front-line employees, that is, the couriers, can provide a satisfactory level of service to the customers, because every day couriers face each of IAT's customers and are frequently seen as the face of the organisation. Their daily job is to pick up packages and deliver them to the customers. The problem was motivating the couriers to give not just satisfactory service but excellent customer service. This is a big problem for the logistics industry generally and the managers of IAT considered that this service focus could be greatly improved by their front-line couriers.

Research by the organisation found that many of the couriers in the industry generally, as well as in IAT, were not very satisfied with their organisation's compensation system, so occasionally problems arose where the couriers gave very bad customer service or demonstrated a very poor attitude during their pickup or delivery of parcels to the customer. The resulting customer complaints caused substantial concern within the company as they considered that a number of contracts could be lost as a result of these grievances.

In an attempt to resolve the problems, senior managers examined the different ways to tackle this issue of poor quality customer service. They found that there were two major reasons that many of the employees were not satisfied with the organisation, and therefore did not provide the level of customer service that was required by the company.

The first reason is that the employees compared their salary with the salary that was paid to the employees of their competitors. This demonstrates a problem with the external equity considerations of the employees. Many thought that their salary was substantially lower than that paid by the competitors of IAT. This could be considered a fault of the compensation system of the organisation. Within the market, IAT does not pay the highest salary nor does it pay the lowest salary; it pays the middle range of the salary level for the industry generally. Therefore, many of the front-line employees were of the opinion that their salary was substantially lower than the employees of their competitors, tending to compare their remuneration with the higher end of the market, even though their actual rate was in the middle, or general market range.

The second reason is the role of internal equity in compensation within the organisation itself. Although all couriers on the front-line have similar jobs, which involve picking up or delivering packages to the customer, the area of delivery for these couriers may be different. Some couriers work in the downtown area of the city, so the delivery time of packages to the customers may be shorter. The courier can then deliver an increased number of packages in a relatively short time frame. However, for many other couriers, their routes will cover country areas and therefore the travel time for these couriers will be substantially longer per package. Also, the customers that these couriers serve are substantially different in their needs and requirements. In the downtown delivery areas, many of the customers are trading companies, but in the remote country areas, many are factory-based. The compensation system, however, for all the couriers, whether they work in the downtown area of the city or delivering and collecting customer packages in remote areas, is the same. Because of the distance and related driving issues, though, it was considered by the employees that the workload of the country couriers was substantially different. Delivering to remote areas places additional strain and stress on the drivers and subsequently, there are a number of safety issues involved that needed to be considered by the company. This is because the couriers need to drive the vehicles for a much longer time period, covering distances of up to 60 or 70 km per delivery, frequently over an hour, whereas in the downtown area, a delivery may only take 10 to 15 minutes per package. Also the factories in the remote areas tend to have bulkier or larger shipments than those of the trading companies in the downtown area. This involves a heavier physical workload for the courier in which some reorganising of the van or truck may be needed after each delivery to ensure that the load is balanced for safety reasons. However, even though all the couriers cover different routes, the compensation system is identical for all the couriers. There is no piece-work salary system for the different couriers, and it is realised that if this was the case, compensation would be more inequitable, favouring the local drivers. It was realised, though, that there was a problem identified with the internal equity in the company, as it relates to the internal compensation system of the organisation and the differing workloads of equivalent-classed staff members. As a result of this inequity, many of the couriers delivering packages to remote areas were not very satisfied with their pay. This is because their income will be comparatively less than those of couriers who deliver parcels to the downtown area, due to the extra workload and effort needed for the remote deliveries. The salary is the same even though there are greater dangers and more problems to those couriers delivering to remote areas.

So to summarise, the comparatively lower salary compared to the competitors of IAT and the perceived inequity of the salary of the compensation system within the organisation have led to the dissatisfaction of some couriers in their current roles within the company. This dissatisfaction with the compensation system in turn has resulted in the couriers offering a bad service to their customers. As a result of this bad service, complaints from customers occurred quite often. Some of the complaints may be that the courier will not wait or that the manner of the courier has been very rude towards the customer. This then results in a big problem for the company. The hardware and support systems of all of the freight companies tend to be identical in that they all have similar methods of delivery, they all have GPS systems within the vehicles and they all charge a similar rate. The only point of difference between the companies, and one which IAT prided itself on, was the aspect of customer service.

The solution

Fortunately, senior management within the organisation realised the impact of the compensation system on the motivation and provision of good quality service to the customers. They investigated possible solutions, which in turn resulted in a number of measures being taken, the prime measure being a pay-for-performance system. Previously the organisation provided a bonus to their employees, paid on a six monthly basis, but recently that was changed to a monthly pay-for-performance system, to more closely tie recognition of good performance with a reward.

Deductions could be made from the new monthly bonus based on four factors. Two of the factors related to customer satisfaction. The first would be a failure in the service provided during normal working hours, such as a missed delivery to the customer. The second would be any effective and valid customer complaint on the service provided by the couriers, such as if the courier was rude to the customer, or refused to collect certain items for delivery. If the employer considers that the criticisms levelled against the courier are justified and that the issue is of sufficient merit, to the extent that it has affected the reputation of the organisation and has a potentially negative effect on the service quality factors, payment will be deducted from the bonus due. If there have been no problems for the relevant period, or it is considered that the complaint is not justified, it is quite possible that the employee will get a 20 per cent pay-for-performance supplement to their usual salary. If any of these indicators demonstrate that a problem has occurred, there may be a deduction made from this pay for performance bonus to the employees. For example, they may only get 10 per cent of the bonus for their performance. It is the role of the local supervisor to decide if the failure in service or complaint lodged is justified. The employee is allowed to present their side of the case if a deduction is to be made.

The other two factors which could have an impact on the couriers' pay, based on their performance, are the issues of safety and punctuality. With the safety issue, if there are any motor accidents caused that are the fault of the employee, a reduction in bonus will occur. With punctuality, if a parcel is promised to be delivered within a certain time span and it is not, with no valid reason being presented by the driver to explain the late delivery, a deduction may occur. The other punctuality issue that would be taken into account is if the driver is continually late to work, thus causing problems in delivery of the parcels. This again could cause a deduction in pay.

Therefore, these four criteria will have an impact, potentially substantial, on each employee's pay. All of the criteria were equally weighted. Additionally the exact date on which an employee received a service failure will be documented and placed on the employee's personal record. This specifically is on the day that a customer complaint was given to the organisation. This, therefore, is one measure that the company has introduced to ensure that customer service improves in what is essentially a service driven company. This change was implemented by the vice president of the Chinese operations and applied to all three regions due to the high level of complaints that were being received.

The responsibility for ensuring that the system works falls on the line manager of the organisation. Every month, the managers are responsible for filling in the performance assessment record of each courier. The line managers themselves are liable to lose their bonus if this task is not completed in a timely manner. This assessment then goes from the line manager to more senior management for their final approval.

For this system to operate efficiently and fairly, the human resources department designed an appropriate form and communicated the requirements of the system to all affected employees to ensure that they were aware of the criteria and the implications on wages. For this form, each of the measurements will be listed. The form was devised to be very user-friendly, to make it easy for the line managers to complete. All they needed to do was to mark on the form at which point the employee's salary bonus should be deducted, with the appropriate service failure and action taken, if necessary.

To date this system has proven quite effective. The front-line employees try their best to avoid a service failure such as a missed pickup or a customer complaint, punctuality has improved and accident occurrences have reduced. This illustrates the effectiveness of the introduced system, with the employees trying to avoid getting a service failure in any of the identified service areas.

The result of the changes

With the introduction of the performance management and incentive system, there has been a major cultural change among the couriers in the company. The end result of the changes has been that there have been a substantially reduced number of complaints coming from the customers about service quality. This is in line with the strategy employed by the company to differentiate its performance from that of the competitors, thus demonstrating its competitive edge in the market. This is through the provision of quality service and improvement to all customers of IAT. The introduction of this system strengthens the company's strategy for becoming a preferred freight delivery organisation in China.

The new system also ties in with external equity issues, in which the salary of the employees can increase by as much as 20 per cent as a result of their bonus. This tends to take the salary of the employees to the higher end of the industry average, and results in their take-home payment being much higher than it was previously, before the incentive system was introduced into the organisation.

Conclusion

Service quality is very important to this organisation to assist it to expand its business and market share. This also allows the organisation to guarantee employee motivation and satisfaction. The philosophy of the organisation was previously based on the two elements of people and profits. However, it has now changed to that of people, service, and profits. It was found that only satisfied employees could offer a good quality service to the customers. Additionally, the acknowledgement of good service and its relationship to increased profit to the company was further realised. This is one of the main measures that the company has taken to improve the satisfaction of its employees, also bringing with it improved customer service. It is hoped that increased customer service and satisfaction will give the company an increase in business. More business, of course, means more profit to the company, with a flow-on to the employees.

This system has been working quite well and has been widely accepted and welcomed by employees of the company. It has resulted in improved staff satisfaction, which has concurrently resulted in improved customer service. The performance and remuneration system has allowed the organisation to integrate human resource practices with the mission and goals of the company, with the added benefit of increased motivation and reduced staff turnover occurring among the couriers.

References

Hochschild, A. (1983) *The Managed Heart: Commercialization of Human Feeling*. Berkeley: University of California Press.

Li Weining and Chen Kangdi (2008) 'Compensation management from the perspective of equity theory', *Market Modernization*, **543**: 312–13.

Liu Yaozhong and Jiang Rongping (2008) 'An empirical analysis on compensation equity', *Psychological Exploration*, **3**: 73–6.

Qiu Weinian (2007) 'Strategies on exploring total compensation to improve job satisfaction', *Market Modernization*, **513**: 276–8.

Shao Meiqiu and Xu Zhongqi (2004) 'Realizing the internal equity in compensation management', *Human Resource Management of China*, **1**: 23–6.

Wang Wei (2004) 'Pay satisfaction and organization equity', *Human Resource Development of China*, **1**: 27–9.

Wu Xiaoyi, Wang Chunxiao and Xie Lishan (2006) 'The effect of equity in compensation management on employee pay satisfaction', *Foreign Economies and Management*, **28**(2): 7–14.

Ye Rensun, Wang Yuqin and Lin Zeyan (2005) 'An empirical study of the impact of job satisfaction and organization commitment on staff turnover in state-owned enterprises', *Management World*, **3**: 122–5.

Zhang Wenxian and Wei Haiyan (2006) 'A study on researches of succession issues in family-owned enterprises in China', *Management Review*, **18**(2): 31–5.

Zhang Xiujuan, Liu Yichen and Shen Wenguo (2007) 'Emotional labor and its motivational factors', *Modern Management Science*, **7**: 37–9.

Zheng Rui and Lu Yutao (2008) 'The impact of non-economic pay and organization equity on pay satisfaction', *Value Engineering*, **2**: 113–15.

Zhou Xuejun and Yi Rong (2004) 'The application of equity theory in compensation management', *Economy and Management*, **18**(12): 50–2.

17

Conclusion

There is growing interest in the management of human resources in the People's Republic of China. There are a number of reasons for this interest, generally led by the view that it can assist in resolving many of the people issues occurring as a result of the increasing number of private, joint and multinational enterprises operating in the country. Based on the findings in the case studies that were researched in 2008 and 2009, the major problem areas are in staff suitability, retention, training, compensation, and management of performance.

This book has covered many of the problems and solutions that have been adopted with mixed success in a number of organisations. Many of the companies, however, are still working on resolving some of the people issues and modifying western practices to suit local cultures, as well as initiating their own unique systems. This allows the opportunity for further research into the dynamic nature of HR in China.

Looking at the major problems and issues that were raised in the research:

1. For a country with a large and diverse population, many companies are having difficulty in finding suitable skilled and trained staff. This is especially noticeable in the large cities, especially Shanghai, but as industry expands into other areas of China, the problem is increasing in view of the expanding economy of the country. There could be a number of aspects causing this problem, including the high expectations of both employers and employees and the reluctance of many companies to provide training to staff if they would not commit to a certain tenure of employment within the company. These issues of both skills and retention of staff, as well as attraction of staff to particular areas to work, which have all been raised in Chapters 4, 5, 9, 10, 11 and 13 could be explored further to develop possible solutions to the problems.

2. It is also evident that in many companies the concept of *guanxi*, which has long been a key concept of industry, may be declining as the consumer society takes hold and employees are more likely to desert their employer in search of better paying work or positions which have, at least in the view of the employee, better 'prospects' for advancement. The move from what was traditionally a collectivist society to an individual focus by an increasing number of employees points to a slow change in the culture and society. One of the companies (Chapter 12) is in contrast, however, with loyalty to the organisation being quite strong as a result of the management practices within the company.

3. Compensation problems were raised in Chapters 7, 13 and 15, and also, as a related performance concern, were mentioned in Chapters 3 and 16. The effect of the economic changes could result in employees being more prepared to leave a company if they have an opportunity to earn more income elsewhere. Furthermore, as highlighted in Chapter 7, the expectation of a guaranteed and equal income for all, despite different performance standards, can result in dissatisfied staff and resulting problems.

4. Finally, a number of other miscellaneous aspects of human resources and related problems were covered in the remaining chapters. The realisation of high staff turnover in Chapter 2 caused the company to develop an effective staff succession system, modified to suit local conditions. Cross-cultural and industrial relations matters were covered in Chapters 4 and 6, with the aspects of a merger and acquisition process being studied in detail in Chapter 6, along with other HR-related concerns and the connected expatriate problems, with resolution (or lack of) noted. The instigation of a good and balanced performance measurement system through the implementation of the balanced scorecard approach, covered in Chapter 8, demonstrates how training and communication can result, among other things, in assisting a company to improve efficiency through reduction of duplication. Better customer service was one of the goals that was achieved through this system. Organisational change, through a joint venture operation, covered in Chapter 14, with the need to change the culture of the employees should be especially noted for the value of overcoming the natural resistance of many staff to the change processes occurring in many companies.

Apart from the specific HR matters raised above, many of the cases also covered other general HR and related management concerns, with a number covering solutions and the result of those solutions, where applicable. This demonstrated the complexity of the HR environment, not only in China but also in other countries. The steps that are being taken to resolve these concerns were also explored.

This book is aimed at both students and academics in Human Resource Management, and International Business, as well as Chinese students of HRM and English. Managers of multinational enterprises and managers who wish to commence business in China would also find this book invaluable to assist in an understanding of Chinese culture and management.

Index